S JESUS GOD?

D1808667

S JESUS GOD?

Examination and Refutation of Popular Cultic Views

Charles G. B. Evans Ph.D.

Outskirts Press, Inc.
Denver, Colorado

Is Jesus God?
An Examination and Refutation of Popular Cultic Views
All Rights Reserved.
Copyright © 2010 Charles G.B. Evans
v3.0 r1.0

Cover designed by Scott F. Barnes

Outskirts Press, Inc.
http://www.outskirtspress.com

ISBN: 978-1-4327-6290-2

Outskirts Press and the "OP" logo are trademarks belonging to Outskirts Press, Inc.

PRINTED IN THE UNITED STATES OF AMERICA

Dedicated to anyone and everyone who has not yet received the Lord Jesus Christ as their personal Saviour, particularly those trapped within the cults.

May the truth of Who Jesus Christ really is become clear to you as you read.

Table of Contents

Foreword

Is Jesus God?

This is a question which has been researched and answered by the author of this excellent thesis. The answer to this question is the most vital capstone to Christianity.

The Deity of the Lord Jesus Christ is one of the most clearly defined doctrines in the Word of God as seen in the following:

(1) The Old Testament proclaims it (Isaiah 7:14). His name is called Immanuel, which is interpreted in the New Testament as meaning God with us (Matthew 1:22-23).

(2) Jesus Christ was proclaimed to be God by angels (Matthew 28:5, 6; Luke 2:10, 11).

(3) Demons acknowledged Him as God (Mark 1:23-27).

(4) Men and women acknowledged Him as Deity (Matthew 14:33; John 11:27; John 20:28, 29).

(5) God the Father acknowledged Him as Deity (Matthew 3:17; Hebrews 1:8, 10).

(6) The Holy Spirit recognized and acknowledged Him as Deity (Mark 12:36).

(7) Jesus also claimed to be God (John 8:58, 59; 10:30; 14:8, 9; Revelation 1:17, 18).

(8) The New Testament declares that Jesus is God (John 1:1; Colossians 2:9). There are many other Scriptures which teach this unquestionable truth, that Jesus is God.

Believing in the Deity of Jesus Christ is what separates true Christians from cultists. The Bible declares that the person who denies the Deity of Jesus Christ is totally without God (1 John 2:22, 23). The person who does not have Christ living in his heart (by the new birth), does not possess God, nor does he have any hope of eternal life (1 John 5:12). Those who deny the Deity of Jesus Christ must also deny the doctrine of the Trinity. There is one God but three personages. All have ascribed to them the attributes of God. For example, God the Father is declared to be God (Deity) (John 8:54). Some of His attributes are seen in such places as Mark 14:36; Acts 17:27 and 2 Timothy 1:9. Jesus Christ is also proclaimed to be God (Deity) in Hebrews 1:8. Some of His attributes (as Deity) are seen in the Scriptures (Hebrews 13:4; Colossians 2:3). The Holy Spirit is also called God (Acts 5:3, 4), and some of His attributes are seen in Psalms 139:7-10; Romans 15:19; 1 Corinthians 2:10, 11 and Hebrews 9:14. The list of Scriptures could go on and on to prove that Jesus is God, but the evidence presented is sufficient. For an in-depth study, I highly recommend reading this great work presented by Charles Evans.

Dr. Cecil Johnson, Ph.D., Th.D., D.D.
President, Christian Bible College

Introduction

TO BE READ

The purpose of this writing is threefold; to present the Biblical teaching on the deity of Jesus Christ, the deity of the Holy Spirit, the existence of the Holy Trinity and the bodily resurrection of the Lord Jesus; to compare said teachings to those of several of the major cults of today; and to better equip the Christian to efficaciously refute those teachings of the cults and isms which diametrically oppose those of the orthodox Christian faith as presented in the Word of God.

To this end, this dissertation is divided into four sections with respective headings as follows: The

Deity of Jesus Christ, The Personality and Deity of the Holy Spirit, The Trinity and The Resurrection of Jesus Christ.

The writings available today on the various cults and isms and their respective beliefs are voluminous, but by no means exhaustive, due to the fact that the beliefs, doctrines and dogmas of the cults tend to change frequently. Therefore, with the intent of presenting a thorough and relatively complete analysis and presentation of the subject, the author has attempted to limit himself to the topics listed in the sub-headings exclusively and entirely.

This is by no means intended to be a complete study of the many varied cults of the world, nor is it a thorough anatomization of the specific cults mentioned herein. Rather, we shall concern ourselves with those teachings of the cults which directly relate to the subject matter of this thesis.

Let it also be understood that the main concern of this work is to effectively present, from a Biblical standpoint, the deity of the Lord Jesus Christ. Neither time nor space allows for a complete refutation of, or response to, the multitudinous theories and assertions of the various cults and isms which deny this cardinal truth of the Christian faith. However, a thorough bibliography has been included which will provide both the interested student, and the curious cultist, with the names and publishers of several books which examine the topic and/or various related topics in greater detail.

It is my hope and prayer that this study will be instrumental in leading many to a true salvation experience with the Living Lord Jesus Christ Who truly is God incarnate.

Charles G.B. Evans
1988

PLEASE NOTE

For the sake of simplicity, the author has chosen to use the common name "Jehovah" when referring to God throughout the text.

However, I wish to point out that this name (Jehovah) is not to be considered the one and only actual name of God, since it (God's actual name) cannot be properly ascertained from the tetragrammaton which consists of the four consonants YHVH and no vowels.

1

The Deity Of Jesus Christ

In the preface to the excellent book, Great Preaching on the Deity of Jesus Christ, Curtis Hudson says,

"When one considers that for nineteen hundred years the deity of Christ has been the cornerstone of the Christian church, it may seem strange that we need to consider at this time the question: WAS CHRIST GOD, OR JUST A MAN? But, even a casual glance through the pages of the religious press – not to speak of the secular press – will convince one that the issue between these two views of the Saviour is a very vital one today.

Many church members – even ministers – openly reject orthodox teachings regarding Christ's personality. In recent times some have come to regard Christ as merely a good man and great teacher. They explain that He was divine in the sense in which all men have something of a divine spark in them. When one departs from his belief in Deity, there is no logical stopping place until he reaches an entire repudiation of Christ as a supernatural Being." [1] (emphasis Hudson's)

It is said that one can be correct in all areas of doctrine or theology and wrong in his beliefs regarding Jesus, and be wrong enough to lose his soul. Can this be? Does it really matter whether or not we believe Jesus is actually God manifested in the flesh, provided we do believe that He is the Saviour, the Christ?

It is the purpose of this study to attempt to answer these questions. But where do we begin?

When first confronted with the challenge to substantiate, from the Scriptures, the deity of Jesus Christ, the author thought it would be a simple task. Armed with the knowledge that the Word of God plainly and clearly spells out that Jesus is indeed God in

1 From the book, GREAT PREACHING ON THE DEITY OF JESUS CHRIST, by Curtis Hutson et al. Sword of the Lord Publishers, Murfreesboro, TN., 1986. Used by permission.

the flesh, it was thought that a basic presentation of two or three straight-forward texts would suffice to answer the challenge. As the reader may know, it just isn't that easy.

There exist several problems confronting one who would present Jesus as God to a cultist. One major example of these difficulties is theological term-switching. In his book, The Kingdom of the Cults, Dr. Walter Martin covers this practice thoroughly in a chapter entitled, "Scaling the Language Barrier".

Dr. Martin has this to say on the subject,

> So it is possible for a Jehovah's Witness, a Christian Scientist or a Mormon, for example, to utilize the terminology of Biblical Christianity with absolute freedom, having already redesigned these terms in a theological framework of his own making and to his own liking, but almost always at direct variance with the historically accepted meanings of the terms. [2]

Martin goes on to explain the complexities of the problem.....

> The vocabulary of the cults is not the vocabulary of the Bible by definition. Only

2 Reprinted by permission from KINGDOM OF THE CULTS by Walter Martin, published and copyright 1985, Bethany House Publishers, Minneapolis, Minnesota 55438. p. 18.

the Lord knows how many fruitless hours have been spent attempting to confront cultists with the claim of the Gospel, when five short minutes of insistence upon definitions of the terms employed in conversation, (particularly concerning the nature of God and the Person, nature and work of Jesus Christ), would have stripped the cult theology of one of its most potent tools, that of theological term-switching.

Through the manipulation of terminology, it is therefore obvious that the cultist has the Christian at a distinct disadvantage, particularly in the realm of the great fundamental doctrines of Biblical theology. [3]

The problem created by term-switching is quite real. For if words have no standard definition and our language is permitted to vary uncontrollably depending on the user, we shall never be able to communicate effectively with those who are lost within the cults.

Again referring to Martin,

The cults capitalize on the almost total inability of the average Christian to understand the subtle art of redefinition in the realm of Biblical theology....Proper usage of definitions as a

3 Reprinted by permission from KINGDOM OF THE CULTS by Walter Martin, published and copyright 1985, Bethany House Publishers, Minneapolis, Minnesota, 55438. p. 19.

practical tool will rob the cultist of at least two of his advantages: surprise and confusion. [4]

The average non-Christian cult owes its very existence to the fact that it has utilized the terminology of Christianity, has borrowed liberally from the Bible, almost always out of context, and sprinkled its format with evangelical clichés and terms wherever possible or advantageous. Up to now this has been a highly successful attempt to represent their respective systems of thought as 'Christian'.

On encountering a cultist then, always remember that you are dealing with a person who is familiar with Christian terminology, and who has carefully redefined it to fit the system of thought he or she now embraces. [5]

The solution to this perplexing problem is far from simple. The Christian must realize that for every Biblical or doctrinal term he mentions, a redefinition light flashes on in the mind of the cultist, and a lightning-fast redefinition is accomplished. Realizing that the cultist will apparently agree with the doctrine under discussion, while firmly disagreeing in reality

4 Reprinted by permission from KINGDOM OF THE CULTS by Walter Martin, published and copyright 1985, Bethany House Publishers, Minneapolis, Minnesota, 55438. p. 19.

5 Ibid. p. 20.

with the historical and Biblical concept, the Christian is on his way to dealing effectively with cult terminology.

This amazing operation of terminological redefinition works very much like a word association test in psychology. [6]

To sum this up then, for example, you may say "Jesus" to a Jehovah's Witness meaning God the Son, the second Person of the Trinity, God in the flesh. However, the Jehovah's Witness is thinking; Jesus – the first creation of Jehovah God, formerly Michael the arch angel, not Jehovah God but a lesser god.

Other problems to be aware of when witnessing to a cultist include misinterpretations, incorrect translations from the original languages of the Bible, inaccurate and/or unorthodox exegesis practices and/or policies of the cults.

It must be stated then, by way of introduction, that to effectively present Jesus to the cults, the Christian must be aware and informed.

It is worth pointing out at this time that although the job of convincing a cultist that Jesus is Who He claimed to be can be most frustrating and quite often appear to be in vain, it is, nonetheless, of

6 Ibid. p. 21.

the utmost importance. Bearing this in mind, the reader is invited to consider the following information remembering at all times that Christianity as a whole depends on nothing more and nothing less than the Person of Jesus Christ.

DOES IT MATTER?

As previously stated, one is tempted to question the importance of accepting or rejecting the teaching of Christ's divinity. Many of the cults willingly and openly teach that Jesus was a very good man, in fact a prophet of the Most High, a perfect example of manhood. Some even go so far as to preach Him as the Son of God (not God the Son, however) and/or the promised Messiah, Saviour or Redeemer. One must ask, isn't this sufficient? After all, Christ is not being rejected by these groups, nor is he being swept aside as a "nobody". Does it really matter whether or not He is accepted as God?

The answer – Yes. Unquestionably so. The most conclusive reasoning behind this affirmative response is the fact that if Jesus Christ was not and is not God, He: a) was wrong and indeed sinful when He received and accepted worship in John 20:28; b) was blasphemous when He thought Himself able to forgive sin in Matthew 9:2, and, c) was blatantly lying when He made claim to Godhood in John 8:58.

2

Was Christ A Sinner?

Those who would choose to deny the deity of the Lord Jesus are carelessly overlooking a very basic Bible doctrine – the sinfulness of ALL mankind (see Psalm 14:3, Romans 3:10, 3:23).

If Jesus be not God, but simply a man, He must have been sinful. For if He was completely sinless, as we know He was, the aforementioned Scriptures which clearly state that ALL have sinned must, of necessity, be incorrect.

However, if Jesus is more than a man, if He is indeed God in the flesh, there is no difficulty in reconciling the difference. Indeed ALL men have sinned, but Jesus, because He is God and not simply a man, was sinless.

So, was Jesus just a man?

We turn to Dr. Herbert Lockyer;

> The Ebionites of the Early Church, and the Uni-
> tarians and Modernists of our time, deny the
> deity of our Lord. To them, He is only a man – a
> good, holy, exemplary man, but only a man.
> Thus, the crown of deity is snatched from His
> brow. But His deity is proven by all He is in Him-
> self, and is able to accomplish.... [7]

Dr. Emery H. Bancroft has this to say;

> If Christ is not deity, He could not have taken
> the place of sinners so as to make atonement
> for their sins. One creature cannot, in the gov-
> ernment of God, take the place of another. An
> angel cannot act in the place of a man, be-
> cause all that angel can do is, on his personal
> account, due to God. This is the universal law
> of creatureship. Or, if allowed to do so, one
> perfect creature could take the place of only
> one sinful creature. It took the deity of Christ to
> give universal value to His death for the race
> and to enable Him 'to taste death for every
> man' (Heb. 2:9). [8]

---

7 Taken from ALL THE DOCTRINES OF THE BIBLE by Herbert Lockyer. Copyright 1964 by the Zondervan Publishing House. Used by permission. p. 45.

8 Taken from ELEMENTAL THEOLOGY, by Emery H. Bancroft. Published by Zondervan Publishers, Grand Rapids, Michigan, 1977, p. 138. With permission of Baptist Bible College & Seminary.

3

Who Would You Send?

The sheer beauty of the Christian faith is that God loved us so very much that He came to save us Himself.

I generally present the concept to a cultist thusly – Picture yourself driving down the street toward your home. As you get closer to your house you notice thick clouds of smoke pouring from the windows and flames dancing along the roof. Suddenly you realize that your family is trapped within the burning house and there is no one there to help them. Now what do you do….a) turn your car around and drive off in an attempt to find someone to save your family, or, b) rush to the house and save your family yourself.

Similarly, suppose your young son or daughter has

fallen into a pond or lake and is struggling vainly to stay at the surface of the water in order to breathe. Once again do you....a) run through the forest in the hopes of finding someone to jump in and save your child, or, b) jump into the water yourself to save your child.

I am sure that in both of the above examples your answer would be "b", you would go yourself. This is no doubt due to your tremendous love and concern for the well-being of your loved ones.

With this in mind, it becomes obviously ludicrous to assume that God "sent someone else" to save us. No, He didn't send another. Because of His great love for His people, He didn't simply send a prophet, a teacher, or living example; He willingly gave up the glory and honor that were rightfully His and came down to earth to suffer and die for us (John 1:14, 1 Timothy 3:16).

To claim that Jesus is not God is to say that God didn't love us enough to come Himself, so He sent someone else. The Bible clearly teaches otherwise.

If Jesus is in fact God Himself, it must be realized that those who deny His deity will have much to answer for at the judgment when they find themselves face to face with the very One they have so vehemently denied (see John 5:22, Acts 10:42, 2 Corinthians 5:10, 2 Timothy 4:1)!

The main aspect and concern of this dissertation is to determine whether or not the Bible teaches anything about Jesus being God.

THOSE WHO DENY IT

Perhaps a short list of the more popular cults which deny the deity of Jesus and/or teach unorthodox opinions of said deity would be beneficial. Such a list would be as follows:

- MORMONS

- JEHOVAH'S WITNESSES

- THE WAY INTERNATIONAL

- HERBERT W. ARMSTRONG'S WORLD-WIDE CHURCH OF GOD

- CHRISTIAN SCIENCE

- UNITY SCHOOL OF CHRISTIANITY

- SCIENTOLOGY

Knowing now the importance of realizing, one way or the other, if Jesus is God, and being knowledge-able regarding which groups claim that He is not, we can and must consider what the Bible has to say about the subject.

It is interesting to note that some cult adherents (e.g. Jehovah's Witnesses) will willingly accept the teachings of the Bible over the teachings of their particular group if they can be shown, beyond a doubt, what the Bible really teaches. This fact is to the Christian's advantage.

Before getting into any great depth with our study, I feel it is an opportune time to echo the words of the great C.I. Scofield.....

> Now I shall feel more comfortable as I go on, if I say at the outset that the merits of my cause should not be judged by my ability in presenting it. Truth itself transcends the ability of any man to present it. All the more, then, if the reasons themselves shall seem to you to be convincing and the proofs shall seem to you to be adequate, will you as honest men be under compulsion to accept them. Give me, then, your attention to that cumulative body of truth which establishes beyond all question this proposition – that Jesus of Nazareth, the historic Christ, was God manifest in the flesh. [9]

At this point nothing could be more helpful or beneficial to the Christian than a thorough hermeneuti-

---

9 From the book, GREAT PREACHING ON THE DEITY OF JESUS CHRIST, by Curtis Hutson, et al. Sword of the Lord Publishers, Murfreesboro, TN., 1986, p. 135. Used by permission.

cal approach to the Scriptures regarding the Person of Christ.

Let us begin with one of the most powerful of all examples – Exodus 3:13, 14. In this familiar passage, the Lord (Jehovah) has appeared unto Moses and commissioned him to go to the children of Israel and deliver them from the rule of Pharaoh. Moses responded with a reasonable question, "…. And they shall say to me, What is his name? What shall I say unto them?"

Now take note of Jehovah's response in verse fourteen for it is of great importance:

> And God said unto Moses, I AM THAT I AM: and he said, Thus shalt thou say unto the children of Israel, I AM hath sent me unto you. (emphasis in the original)

One must consider the magnitude of this title in order to fully appreciate its significance. Although it contains many meanings, the one we are concerned with for this study is the fact that everything is contained in this name. The Lord made no attempt to explain Who He is, where He is, why He is, etc. Rather, all was summed up in the title He gave unto Himself – I AM.

Keeping the above in mind, consider the eighth chapter of the Gospel of John. Beginning with verse fifty-one, we see that Jesus was talking with the Jews and, as usual, they were not happy about the things He was saying. This discomfort on the part of the Jews was culminated when Christ made a comment regarding Abraham (vs. 56, 57). When the Jews sarcastically challenged Jesus about His ability to have known Abraham since he (Abraham) had long since died, Jesus provided this self-explanatory response: "Verily, verily I say unto you, Before Abraham was, I AM" (v. 58, emphasis mine).

That Jesus was claiming to be the I AM (Jehovah) of Exodus 3:14 is obvious. Those who would argue against this fact are directed to the following verse (59) wherein we learn that the Jews fully understood the context in which Christ was speaking. So clear to them was the message of Christ's claim that they did the only thing any self-respecting Jew could do to one who claimed to be God – they prepared to stone Him to death! It must be understood that the Jews were thoroughly familiar with the account of the exodus of their forefathers from Egypt. They were well aware of the communication between Moses and Jehovah on Sinai. They knew that Jehovah had called Himself the I AM. Therefore, in their way of thinking, anyone claiming to be the I AM was claiming to be Jehovah and anyone claiming to be Jehovah was nothing more than a blasphemer who must be put to death.

It is imperative that the underlying implications of

the above account be fully realized by the cultist. If, as the cults are so fond of teaching, Jesus was not making a claim to be the I AM of the Old Testament, the ramifications of His statement of verse fifty-eight would not have included the attempted murder (stoning) of verse fifty-nine. Jesus called Himself Jehovah and the Jews responded in the only way they could to a "mere man" Who called Himself God.

Further proof that Jesus did indeed claim to be God, as well as that the Jews of His day fully understood His claim, can be found in John 10:31-33. Once again the Jews proceeded to attempt to stone Jesus and when He plainly asked them why they were going to kill Him, they answered, "...Because that thou, being a man, MAKEST THYSELF GOD" (emphasis mine).

I have had Jehovah's Witnesses tell me, on more than one occasion, that the Jews merely claimed that Jesus professed to be equal with Jehovah, but that they were mistaken. They (the Jehovah's Witnesses) say that Jesus never actually claimed this equality – the Jews erroneously thought that He did.

When ruminating this assertion we must bear one thing in mind; to claim to be God or to claim equality with Him is surely the lowest form of blasphemy. Therefore, if Jesus had been accused of this and in fact He was not God and did not claim to be, He most assuredly would have defended Himself against such strong charges or at least attempted to point out that He was not actually saying what the Jews thought He was saying.

But we do not see this. Rather, in every instance, Jesus allowed the Jews to continue thinking that He had claimed divinity – Because He had!

With the above in mind, we can only conclude that Jesus was lying, mistaken, insane, OR He really is Who He said He is.

Before going further in our Scripture analysis, it would be good to consider the questions brought about by the aforementioned references (John 8:58, 59; 10:31-33).

Why were the religious leaders so frequently upset with Christ?

Why did they oppose Him so vehemently? Why did they have Him killed? These questions can be answered with a singular statement – Because He called Himself God.

Thinking in this regard, one cannot help but won-der....Would those cults which deny the Godship of Jesus today put Him to death as the religious lead-ers of the day did? Of course, they would be quick to answer in the negative, and we would like to agree, but one must admit that the Jehovah's Witnesses, The Way International, and others, share one very common trait with those of the First Century which arranged the crucifixion of Jesus....they each deny and reject the fact that Jesus Christ is Jehovah God!

4

The Word Is God

With no attempt to appear chronological, let us now turn to one of the most mistranslated, misinterpreted, misunderstood Bible verses on the topic, John 1:1. In the beginning was the WORD, and THE WORD WAS WITH GOD, and THE WORD WAS GOD (emphasis mine).

As the reader can quickly ascertain, this verse clearly expresses the fact that Jesus was with Jehovah in the beginning, and, more than that, Jesus (the Word) was (is) God!

Needless to say, because of the straightforward, unquestionable message of this passage, the various cults in question find it necessary to augment or in some cases change the rendering or the context of the verse claiming a discrepancy between the modern translations and the original languages.

Due to the fact that this verse is capable of "making or breaking" the doctrine of Christ's deity, the opportunity for a fairly detailed analysis of the passage cannot be passed by.

Let us first examine the verse in question by allowing Scripture to interpret Scripture. We first learn that, "In the beginning was the Word". This phrase is illuminated when cross-referenced with 1 John 1:1, 2;

> That which was from the beginning, which we have heard, which we have seen with our eyes, which we have looked upon, and our hands have handled, of the Word of life; (for the life was manifested, and we have seen it, and bear witness, and shew unto you that eternal life, WHICH WAS WITH THE FATHER, and was manifested unto us). (emphasis mine)

It should be obvious that this passage, like John 1:1, is referring to Christ for it is common knowledge to the Bible student that the Father was never "looked upon" nor "handled". Also, we see from the latter portion of the previously quoted

Scripture that the Word was with the Father. It is not necessary to explain the absurdity of saying, "the Father was with the Father". The only conclusion then is that the Word was indeed WITH the Father IN THE BEGINNING, but is not actually the Father.

Turning back to the Gospel of John we learn that it verifies what was said in 1 John 1:2, "And the Word was made flesh, and dwelt among us..."(1:14). Once again, an explanation should not be required. We know that the Father Himself was never "made flesh". Rather, Jesus (The Word) took on the form of a human man and came to live on the earth two thousand years ago.

This teaching is further promulgated by a Scripture which spells things out so clearly it cannot be contested; 1Timothy 3:16...

> And without controversy great is the mystery of godliness: GOD WAS MANIFEST IN THE FLESH (Jesus), justified in the Spirit, seen of angels, preached unto the Gentiles, believed on in the world, received up into glory. (brackets and emphasis mine)

As we've already noted, the Father was never "manifest in the flesh". Simple logistics tell us that, according to this passage, Jesus is God. Please also note that Acts 1:9 teaches that it was Jesus Who, as in the above quoted Scripture, was "received up into glory".

The second or middle teaching of John 1:1 is that, "The Word was with God". The seventeenth chapter of the same Gospel shares more than one Scripture which supports the belief that the Word, or Jesus, was with the Father in the beginning. Reading verse five we learn of the instance when Jesus Himself said,

> And now, O Father, glorify thou me with thine own self with the glory WHICH I HAD WITH THEE BEFORE THE WORLD WAS. (emphasis mine)

Verse twenty-four echoes this with,

> ....For thou lovedst me (Jesus) BEFORE THE FOUNDATION OF THE WORLD. (brackets and emphasis mine)

The reader should consider the fact that Jesus plainly and clearly declared that He shared God's glory "BEFORE THE WORLD WAS" but Isaiah quotes Jehovah as saying,

> "I am Jehovah. That is my name; and to NO ONE ELSE SHALL I GIVE MY OWN GLORY...." (42:8 NWT emphasis mine)

Obviously Jesus could not be "someone else" for if He was, He would not have been permitted to share Jehovah's glory. Jesus must be Jehovah Himself in order to have Jehovah's glory.

5
Jesus Is The Creator

Risking the possibility of confusing the issue, it is indeed an opportune time to consult various Scriptures which further prove that Jesus was indeed with the Father in the beginning by expressing the role He (Jesus) played in the creation of the world.

Colossians 1 teaches that,

> By Him (Jesus) were all things created, that are in heaven, and that are in earth, visible and invisible, whether they be thrones, or dominions, or principalities, or powers: ALL THINGS WERE CREATED BY HIM, and for him: AND HE IS BEFORE ALL THINGS, and

by him all things consist. (vs. 16, 17, brackets and emphasis mine)

The Book of Hebrews also teaches that Christ is the Creator by stating,

God...hath in these last days spoken unto us by His son (Jesus) .... BY WHOM ALSO HE MADE THE WORLDS; (1:1, 2, brackets and emphasis mine).

We know now that Jesus is the Creator, but the first verse of the Bible says, "In the beginning GOD CREATED..." (Genesis 1:1, emphasis mine)

Dr. John Rice offers the following:

'In the beginning' (vs. 1), that is, in the beginning of this universe and before. The first three words in this chapter are the same as the first three words in Genesis; and these first five verses talk about the same time and events as the first chapter of Genesis. Jesus was there Himself and had part in creation. When God said, 'Let us make man' (Gen. 1:26), He certainly included Himself, Jesus and the Holy Spirit. Jesus is as old as God the Father. He is deity. So He could say, 'Before Abraham was, I am' (8:58). He is 'the Ancient of Days' of Daniel 7:9, 10 with white hair like wool. That Scripture tells of One ruling and judging; and all judgment is given to the Son.

When Jesus healed the woman physically older than He, the woman with an issue of blood for twelve years, He addressed her, 'Daughter' (Matt. 9:22; Mark 5:34; Luke 8:48). He is older than any man; He is eternal God. So He 'was in the beginning with God' (vs. 2). Wherever God was before creation, Christ was there with Him. [10]

Is Jesus God? Let us continue our study.

The Watchtower submits that Jehovah God created Jesus first and then created everything else "through" Him [11] This theory does not stand up to proper exegetical practices when Isaiah 64:8 is considered;

And now, O Jehovah, you are our Father. We are the clay, and you are our Potter; and all of us are the work OF YOUR HAND (NWT, emphasis mine).

The assertion becomes even less acceptable in the light of Isaiah 44:24;

10 From the book, GREAT PREACHING ON THE DEITY OF JESUS CHRIST, by Curtis Hutson, et al. Sword of the Lord Publishers, Murfreesboro, TN., 1986, p. 135. Used by permission.

11 Let God be True. Watchtower Bible and Tract Society, Brooklyn, New York (revised edition), 1953, p. 33.

> This is what JEHOVAH has said, your Re-
> purchaser and THE FORMER OF YOU from
> the belly: 'I, JEHOVAH, AM DOING EV-
> ERYTHING, stretching out the heavens BY
> MYSELF, laying out the earth. WHO WAS
> WITH ME?' (NWT, emphasis mine)

The same verse reads as follows in the King James Version;

> Thus saith the Lord, they redeemer, and HE
> THAT FORMED THEE FROM THE WOMB,
> I am the Lord THAT MAKETH ALL THINGS;
> that stretcheth forth the heavens ALONE;
> that spreadeth abroad the earth BY MY-
> SELF...(emphasis mine)

No lengthy commentary is necessary for the above. The Scripture makes it quite simple. Several verses which we have already considered teach that Jesus is the Creator. The Witnesses claim that yes, Jesus was in fact the Creator but Jehovah Himself created "through" Jesus. The Word of God responds, even when the Watchtower's own New World Transla- tion is used, by stating that Jehovah created ALL THINGS, BY HIMSELF (ALONE). The only possible conclusion – Jesus is Jehovah.

Still concentrating on John 1:1, we have ascer- tained that Jesus existed in the beginning and we also know that He was with the Father. Let's now

plicitly or explicitly. If this verse was supposed to be speaking of Jesus Christ as the Logos (Word) merely in God's foreknowledge, or thought, then why didn't John write, 'In the beginning was God, and the thought was with God, and God was God'? John did not write it that way because that is not what Scripture teaches. [13]

The author finds the translation according to Wierwille particularly offensive in the light of a personal letter received from a top representative of The Way International which was sent in response to the author's questions regarding John 1:1. The letter, dated March 20, 1987, states that the Greek word logos is accepted "for its literal meaning", rather than any theological INTERPOLATIONS connected with it.[14] (emphasis mine)

After noting that Wierwille added TWELVE NEW WORDS INTO THE TEXT in question, it is fascinating to hear The Way's representative claim that they are not interested in interpolations!

One example then of how cults cover up verses which disagree with their theology is to alter them, with no regard whatsoever to the original, God-inspired meaning.

---

13 The New Cults by Walter R. Martin. Regal Books, Ventura, CA., 1980, p. 59.

14 Letter to author from The Way International Headquarters dated March 20, 1987.

Another interesting example of Scriptural sabotage can be found in the Watchtower organization (Jehovah's Witnesses). The Witnesses too have seen fit to change the context of the verse basing their actions on "Greek scholarship". According to the Watchtower John 1:1 should read as follows:

> In (the) beginning the Word was, and the Word was with God, and the Word was a god. (brackets in the original)

Academically the New World Translation rendering of the verse is mendacious. Greek scholar after Greek scholar, some Christian, others not, have cogently denied and rejected it as nothing short of a blatant falsehood. Yet the Watchtower holds to it.

Arthur M. Bowser approaches the subject thusly:

> The reasoning seems to be that since the Greek word 'God' (theos) does not have the definite article, it must be translated indefinitely as 'a god'. This, however, overlooks a very important Greek rule known as Colwell's rule which states, 'The absence of the article does not make the predicate indefinite or qualitative when it precedes the verb.' In contrast, when the predicate noun comes after the verb, the definite article must be used to make the noun definite.

> Even a casual look at the Greek text in John 1 shows that the predicate 'God' precedes the verb 'was' and consequently the testimony of John is that 'the Word was God'. [15] (brackets Bowser's)

Ratiocinatively the translation is no better, for it is the Witnesses themselves who are so fond of quoting Isaiah 44:6,

> This is what Jehovah has said, The King of Israel and the Repurchaser of him, Jehovah of armies, 'I am the first and I am the last, and BESIDES ME THERE IS NO GOD'... (NWT emphasis mine)

Even when their own translation is used, the Witnesses have boxed themselves into a corner. Either Isaiah 44:6 is incorrect, or their translation of John 1:1 is a lie. For how can Jesus be "a god" if Jehovah Himself declares, "Besides me THERE IS NO GOD"? (See also 43:10)

This point can be taken further. Simple reasoning shows us that if Jesus is not Jehovah but a "lesser god" (as the Watchtower asserts), He (Jesus) must be a false god since Scripture clearly states that Jehovah is the ONE TRUE GOD in the following passages;

---

15 What Every Jehovah's Witness Should Know. Arthur M. Bowser. Used by permission, Accent Publications, Denver, Colorado, 1978, p. 57.

Now for a long season Israel hath been without THE TRUE GOD. 2 Chronicles 15:3

But the Lord is THE TRUE GOD, he is the living God. Jeremiah 10:10

Master, thou hast said the truth: for there is ONE GOD; and there is none other but he. Mark 12:32

And this is life eternal, that they might know thee THE ONLY TRUE GOD... John 17:3

....and that there is NONE OTHER GOD BUT ONE. 1 Corinthians 8:4

....and how ye turned to God from idols to serve the living AND TRUE GOD. 1 Thessalonians 1:9

For there is ONE GOD... 1 Timothy 2:5

Thou believest that there is ONE GOD; thou doest well. James 2:19

....This is THE TRUE GOD... 1 John 5:20

See also Deuteronomy 4:35, 39; Isaiah 43:10; 44:6; 45:5, 18, 21, 22; 46:9 (emphasis in all above Scripture is mine)

Needless to say, if something isn't true, it is false. There is no middle ground. Similarly, if Jehovah is THE ONLY TRUE GOD, and if (according to the Watchtower), Jesus is not Jehovah but is a lesser god, He absolutely must be a false god! Of course this is unthinkable.

Jesus is true because He IS Jehovah!

The Church of Jesus Christ of Latter-Day Saints (Mormons) has still another way of handling the predicament. Although they claim to believe and accept the Bible as truth, along with their own Book of Mormon, they unashamedly ignore each and every passage from BOTH books which oppose their own distinct theology!

Much more could be said about each of these cults. However, having made my point, I think it best to return to the matter at hand.

6

Jesus Is "The Mighty God"

Another convincingly puissant portion of Scripture which clearly and explicitly teaches the deity of Christ is Isaiah 9:6. As the reader may know, the Old Testament Book of Isaiah is prophetic in nature and essence. The particular prophecy we wish to examine here is referring to the coming of the Messiah;

> For unto us a child is born, unto us a son is given: and the government shall be upon his shoulder: and his name shall be called Wonderful, Counsellor, THE MIGHTY GOD, The Everlasting Father, The Prince of Peace. (emphasis mine)

Who is this child, this Son? Who is The Prince of Peace? Even Biblical abcedarians do not question the identity of the One described by Isaiah. He is none other than Jesus of Nazareth.

Before proceeding let me caution the reader to keep the aforementioned verse in its proper, God-intended context. The entire verse is speaking of Jesus. It is He Who would be called Wonderful, Counsellor, MIGHTY GOD, Everlasting Father, and The Prince of Peace. One would show highly questionable study and/or research methods if suggesting that part of the verse speaks of Jesus while another speaks of the Father.

One may wish to lovingly point out to Jehovah's Witnesses that their own New World Translation of the verse in question is strikingly similar to the King James Version;

> For there has been a child born to us, there has been a son given to us; and the princely rule will come to be upon his shoulder. And his name will be called Wonderful Counsellor, MIGHTY GOD, Eternal Father, Prince of Peace. (NWT emphasis mine)

Let the reader be informed that the Witnesses themselves have said that this verse is speaking of Jesus! [16]

---

16 AWAKE! Magazine. February 8, 1987, Vol. 68, No. 3. Watchtower Bible and Tract Society, p. 26.

Turning to the Book of Acts we find another stunningly corroborative reference to the equality of the Father and the Son;

> Take heed therefore unto yourselves, and to all the flock, over which the Holy Ghost hath made you over-seers, to feed the church OF GOD, which HE hath purchased with HIS OWN BLOOD. (20:28, emphasis mine)

Of course, it is common knowledge that Jesus, the Son, was the Lamb of God, the sacrifice Who suffered and shed HIS BLOOD to wash away the sin of the world (John 1:29). But this Scripture teaches us that GOD purchased the Church with HIS OWN BLOOD! There is no contradiction here... The blood of Jesus IS the blood of God because Jesus IS God!

This same aspect of the Father and the Son being equal parts of the same Jehovah God can be seen in Zechariah 2:8-11;

> For thus saith the LORD of hosts; After the glory hath he sent me unto the nations which spoiled you: for he that toucheth you toucheth the apple of his eye. For, behold, I will shake mine hand upon them, and they shall know that the LORD of hosts hath sent me. Sing and rejoice, O daughter of Zion: for, lo, I come, and I will dwell in the midst

of thee, saith the LORD. And many nations shall be joined to the LORD in that day, and shall be my people: and I will dwell in the midst of thee, and thou shalt know that the LORD of hosts hath sent me unto thee. (emphasis in the original)

Careful reading of the above verses will reveal that Jehovah actually sent Jehovah!

Similarly we find that John the Baptist was directly commissioned by Jehovah to prepare the way before Himself. This is evident simply by cross-referencing the following passages:

The voice of him that crieth in the wilderness, Prepare ye the way of the LORD, make straight in the desert a highway FOR OUR GOD.... Isaiah 40:3

Behold, I will send my messenger, and he shall prepare the way BEFORE ME.... Malachi 3:1

....and realizing the axiomatic fact that John the Baptist actually prepared the way FOR CHRIST (See Matthew 3:1 – 3-; Mark 1:1 – 8; Luke 3:1 – 4; John 1:6 – 8).

So what conclusion do we reach? Does the Word of God contradict itself by stating in the Old Testament that the messenger would prepare the way before Jehovah while the New Testament plainly teaches that he prepared the way for Jesus? Or, is there an error in the Word of God? Or, are all of the aforementioned Scriptures accurate and correct because Jesus is God?

Since the first two assertions must be rejected, we find ourselves once again confronted with the fact of Christ's deity.

7

Scripture Supports Scripture

The tremendous value of allowing Scripture to support Scripture cannot be over-emphasized. This great merit is easily recognized in the above example as well as in the following:

In the Gospel of John, Jesus is quoted as saying, 'If any man thirst, let him come unto me, and drink' (7:37).

Earlier in John's account we read a similar statement which was made by Jesus to the Samaritan woman at the well....

If thou knewest the gift of God, and who it is that saith to thee, give me to drink;

> thou wouldest have asked of him, and
> he would have given thee living water.
> (4:10)

These verses take on considerable consequence when considered along with a similar passage in the Revelation. The Alpha and Omega (Jesus, according to chapter one) has this to say,

> I will give unto him that is athirst of the fountain of the water of life freely. He that overcometh shall inherit all things; AND I (Jesus) WILL BE HIS GOD.... (21:6, 7, brackets and emphasis mine)

As Dr. Jack Van Impe points out in his excellent book, Great Salvation Themes [17], Paul and Silas directed the inquiring Philippian jailor to "Believe on THE LORD JESUS CHRIST, and thou shalt be saved, and thy house" (Acts 16:31, emphasis mine). But just a little further along in the chapter we learn that the jailor believed IN GOD with all his house! (See v. 34)

The two passages, taken together, demonstrate that belief in the Lord Jesus is synonymous with belief in God!

---

17 Great Salvation Themes, Jack Van Impe. Jack Van Impe Ministries, Royal Oak, Michigan, pgs. 21-22.

THOMAS CALLED JESUS GOD

More proof? No sooner requested than offered – John 20:28. Thomas had refused to believe that Jesus had risen from the dead until he himself could touch the nail prints in His hands and the hole in His side. When the risen Lord gave him the opportunity to do just that, he immediately exclaimed,

"My Lord AND MY GOD" (emphasis mine).

Many cultists attempt to explain Thomas' acclamation by asserting that he called Christ his Lord but then looked heavenward (to the Father) and said, "...and my God". However, the Bible plainly says, "And Thomas answered and said UNTO HIM (Jesus)" (brackets and emphasis mine). No mention is made of Thomas saying one thing to Jesus and another to the Father. No hint is provided of Thomas looking toward heaven before addressing God (this verse is also sufficiently intact in the New World Translation).

THE FULLNESS OF THE GODHEAD IN JESUS

Colossians 2:9 teaches that ALL THE FULLNESS of the Godhead dwells bodily in Jesus. The reader will note that it does not read, "a portion" or "a small amount" or "some of", but ALL THE FULLNESS of the Godhead.

If a dress is white, blue and yellow, it is white AND blue AND yellow. But if a dress is ALL blue or FULLY blue, then it is blue! If a boat is wood, metal and plastic, it is wood AND metal AND plastic. But if a boat is ALL wood or FULLY wood, then it is wood! If ALL the FULLNESS of the Godhead dwells in Jesus, He IS God.

THE FATHER KNOWS WHO JESUS REALLY IS!

Another way of looking at this concept is provided in the first chapter of the Book of Hebrews. Does the Father lie? Does He ever make a mistake? Of course not. Therefore, He must have been truthful and correct when He addressed His Son (Jesus) as God.

> "But unto the Son he saith, Thy throne, O GOD, is for ever and ever...." (vs. 8, emphasis mine).

A second teaching on the subject is found in verse six where we learn that the Father told all of the angels to worship Jesus. This may not seem to add significantly to this study, but when one realizes that God does not make mistakes or changes in His way of doing things, one can reach only one conclusion concerning Christ's divinity when the above is cross-referenced with the following:

> And the devil said unto him (Jesus), All this power will I give thee, and the glory of them: for that is delivered unto me; and to whomsoever I will I give it. If thou therefore wilt worship me, all shall be thine. And Jesus answered and said unto him, Get thee behind me, Satan: for it is written, Thou shalt worship THE LORD THY GOD, AND HIM ONLY shalt thou serve. (Luke 4:6-8, brackets and emphasis mine)

> And I John saw these things, and heard them, and when I had heard and seen, I fell down to worship before the feet of the angel which showed me these things. Then saith he unto me, SEE THOU DO IT NOT: for I am thy fellow servant, and of thy brethren the prophets, and of them which keep the sayings of this book: WORSHIP GOD. (Revelation 22:8, 9; emphasis mine)

The message of the above Scriptures is clear. Jehovah is the only Being in existence Who is rightfully deserving of worship. Jesus Himself said so in Luke, chapter four. Yet the Father commanded all of His angels to worship Jesus. This leaves us with only two possible conclusions: 1) The Father changed His way of doing things and went against what He had previously said and decided it was acceptable for someone other than Himself to be worshiped, or, 2) Jesus is God and therefore He is worthy of worship. The Bible student will immediately recognize the foolishness of the first assertion based on several Scriptures which indicate the immutability of God, including Malachi 3:6; Hebrews 13:8; James 1:17; 1 Peter 1:24, 25.

With the first suggestion shown to be quite impossible, we are left with only one alternative – Jesus was worshiped because of Who He is – God (See also Matthew 8:2; 9:18; 14:33; 15:25; 28:9; Luke 5:8; 24:52; John 20:28).

We concur with Dr. William Evans;

> The homage given to Christ in these scriptures would be nothing short of sacrilegious idolatry if Christ were not God. There seemed to be not the slightest reluctance on the part of Christ in the acceptance of such worship. Therefore either Christ was God or He was an imposter. But His whole life refutes the idea of imposture. It was He who said, 'Worship God only'; and He had no right to take the place of God if He were not God. [18]

---

18 Taken from THE GREAT DOCTRINES OF THE BIBLE by William Evans (enlarged edition). Used by permission, Moody Bible Institute of Chicago, Ill., 1974. p. 60.

PETER CALLED JESUS GOD

Still another illuminative verse is found in 2 Peter,

> ....To them that have obtained like precious faith with us through the righteousness of GOD AND OUR SAVIOUR JESUS CHRIST. (1:1, emphasis mine)

The cults are quick to assert that the writer is speaking of two individuals, God (the Father), and Jesus Christ. But is this actually the case? Again referring to Bowser, we read;

> The Apostle Peter begins his second epistle by rejoicing in the salvation which has been made personally available 'through the righteousness of God and our Saviour Jesus Christ'. Your (Jehovah's Witnesses) translators take this to mean that Peter is distinguishing between the righteousness of God and that of a distinct person, the Saviour. Such a rendering, however, overlooks another basic Greek rule, known since 1798 as Granville Sharp's rule. Mr. Sharp states that 'when the copulative 'and' connects two nouns of the same case, if the article precedes the first noun and is not repeated before the second noun, the latter always refers to the same person that is expressed

or described by the first noun. [19] (brackets mine)

Consequently we see that Peter was not writing of two separate individuals, but one – God.

19 What Every Jehovah's Witness Should Know. Arthur M. Bowser. Used by permission, Accent Publications, Denver, Colorado, 1978, pgs. 59-60.

8
Who Is The First
And The Last?

Once again let me encourage you to consider the forty-fourth chapter of Isaiah. In verse six we read,

> Thus saith the Lord the King of Israel, and His redeemer the Lord of hosts; I AM THE FIRST, AND I AM THE LAST; and beside me THERE IS NO GOD. (emphasis mine)

As we have already seen, this particular passage completely extirpates the New World Translation rendering of John 1:1, but let's delve ever deeper into the Scriptures and see what else we can learn about this First and Last Who, by His own declaration, is THE ONLY GOD.

Most students are aware that the Book of the Revelation also mentions the Lord and addresses Him as the First and the Last. Let us consider what is said. The first chapter provides us with the following;

> I AM ALPHA AND OMEGA, THE BEGIN-
> NING AND THE ENDING, saith THE
> LORD, which is, and which was, and which
> is to come, THE ALMIGHTY. (v. 8, emphasis
> mine).

The Jehovah's Witnesses are firm in their belief that this passage is speaking of none other than Jehovah God and I certainly concur with them on this point, but let's go a little further.

Beginning with verse eleven of the same chapter we find this statement, "....I AM ALPHA AND OME-GA, THE FIRST AND THE LAST" (emphasis mine). Jumping down to verse thirteen, we read a vivid description of the One Who is speaking and calling Himself the FIRST AND THE LAST (of course we already know the identity of the One Who is speaking. He is Jehovah. We have ascertained this by studying the 'pet' Scripture of the Watchtower, Isaiah 44:6);

> And in the midst of the seven candlesticks
> one like unto the Son of man, clothed with
> a garment down to the foot, and girt about

the paps with a golden girdle. His head and his hairs were white like wool, as white as snow; and his eyes were as a flame of fire; and his feet like unto fine brass, as if they burned in a furnace; and his voice as the sound of many waters.

This description can also be found in the Old Testament Book of Daniel (7:9) where the One being described is referred to as the Ancient of Days; this is, of course, Jehovah God. Continuing our reading in chapter one of the Revelation, John describes his own reaction,

And when I saw him, I fell at his feet as dead. And he laid his right hand upon me, saying unto me, Fear not; I AM THE FIRST AND THE LAST. (emphasis mine)

Again I point out that we have already affirmed by proper methods of Biblical exegesis that the First and Last is Jehovah; but if we read the following verse, the teaching of the Watchtower is shattered once again:

I am he that liveth, AND WAS DEAD; and, behold, I am alive forevermore, Amen; and have the keys of hell and of death. (v. 18, emphasis mine)

The Father was never dead. This goes without

saying. Yet this Scripture clearly states that the One Who was dead is known as the First and the Last, an Individual Whom we know is Jehovah!

As if this weren't enough evidence, the Book of Revelation offers still more proof for the deity of Jesus in the last chapter. Verses seven and twelve begin with the same words, "Behold, I come quickly". But Who is "coming quickly"? We find the answer to this question in the next verse (13),

> I am Alpha and Omega, the beginning and the end, THE FIRST AND THE LAST" (emphasis mine). But verse sixteen makes the identity of the One Who is coming quickly clearer still, "I JESUS...." (emphasis mine). And again the message of the Lord's quick return is reiterated in verse twenty along with further evidence that we are indeed reading of Jesus; He which testifieth these things saith, Surely I come quickly. Amen. Even so, come, LORD JESUS" (emphasis mine).

9

Who Raised Jesus
From The Dead?

Another forthright example of Christ's oneness with the Father is demonstrated in His resurrection. Acts 3:26 says,

> "Unto you first GOD, HAVING RAISED UP HIS SON Jesus...." (emphasis mine).

While 1 Thessalonians 1:10 says,

> "....And to wait for his Son from heaven, whom HE RAISED FROM THE DEAD, even Jesus...." (emphasis mine).

But John 2:19 and 21 declare,

> "JESUS answered and said unto them, Destroy this temple, and in three days I WILL RAISE IT UP...He spake of the temple of his body" (emphasis mine).

Is there a contradiction here? How can the Bible teach in one place that the Father raised Jesus from the dead while also teaching that Christ raised Himself from the dead? The answer is found in Acts 2:24 where we learn that GOD raised Jesus!

In other words, all of the aforementioned Scriptures are correct and in perfect harmony with one another. Both the Father AND Christ raised Jesus from the dead because they are both one in the same God.

10
Attributes And Titles Shared By Jesus And The Father

Another method of demonstrating Christ's deity to the cultist is by ruminating the attributes and titles which both Jesus and the Father share. Understandably, one should not be required to explain that there are several qualities attributed to Jehovah which are His alone. With this in mind we shall examine several passages of Scripture which express rather interesting teachings.

First of all, Genesis 1:1; Isaiah 40:28; and Isaiah 44:24 all teach that Jehovah is the Creator;

> In the beginning GOD CREATED the heaven and the earth.

THE EVERLASTING GOD, the Lord, THE CREATOR of the ends of the earth... I am the Lord THAT MAKEST ALL THINGS; that stetcheth forth the heavens ALONE; that spreadeth abroad the earth BY MY-SELF. (emphasis in above Scriptures mine)

See also Psalm 100:3; Isaiah 19:25; 29:23; 42:5; 43:7; 45:11 and 12; Zechariah 12:1.

But John 1:3; Colossians 1:16, 17; and Hebrews 1:1 and 2 teach that Jesus is the Creator;

ALL THINGS WERE MADE BY HIM (Jesus); and without him was not anything made that was made.

For by him (Jesus) WERE ALL THINGS CREATED, that are in heaven, and that are in earth...ALL THINGS WERE CRE-ATED BY HIM, and for him.

God...Hath in these last days spoken unto us by his Son (Jesus)...BY WHOM ALSO HE MADE THE WORLDS. (brackets and emphasis in above Scriptures mine)

Isaiah 43:11; 45:22 and Hosea 13:4 all teach that Jehovah is the only Saviour;

> I, even I, am the Lord; and beside me THERE IS NO SAVIOUR.

> Look unto me, AND BE YE SAVED...For I am God, and there is NONE ELSE.

> I am the Lord THY GOD...THERE IS NO SAVIOUR BESIDE ME.

But Luke 2:11 and John 4:42 teach that Jesus is the Saviour; [20]

> For unto you is born this day in the city of David A SAVIOUR, WHICH IS CHRIST THE LORD.

> ....This is indeed the Christ, THE SAVIOUR OF THE WORLD. (all emphasis mine)

In Jeremiah 17:10 Jehovah is portrayed as One Who "searches the heart";

> I the Lord search the heart, I try the reins, even to give to every man according to his ways, and according to the fruit of his doings.

But this very same description is applied to Jesus in Revelation 2:23;

---

20 Note: The Jehovah's Witnesses claim that Jehovah is the only Saviour and that Christ's title of Saviour does not make Him equal with Jehovah anymore than others who are addressed by the same title within Scripture (see 2 Kings 13:5 and Nehemiah 9:27). However, they overlook the important detail that ONLY Christ and Jehovah are set forth as the Saviour of all mankind or "the world".

> I (Jesus) am he which searcheth the reins and hearts: and I will give unto every one of you according to your works.

Isaiah 8:13, 14 sets forth Jehovah as the stumbling block;

> Sanctify the Lord of hosts himself; and let him be your fear, and let him be your dread.

> And he shall be for a sanctuary; BUT FOR A STONE OF STUMBLING and for a ROCK OF OFFENCE to both the houses of Israel, for a gin and for a snare to the inhabitants of Jerusalem.

But Peter, when writing of Christ, refers to Him as the stumbling block (1 Peter 2:8);

> ...and a STONE OF STUMBLING, AND A ROCK OF OFFENCE...*

PSALM 23 sets forth God as the Shepherd;

> Jehovah is my SHEPHERD. (NWT)

While John 10:11 and 10:14 present Christ as the Shepherd;

---

* All brackets and emphasis contained in Scripture references are the author's unless otherwise indicated.

I (Jesus) am the good SHEPHERD.

I (Jesus) am the good SHEPHERD, and know my sheep.

But Ezekiel 34:23 and John 10:15 both state that there is but ONE SHEPHERD;

And I will set up ONE SHEPHERD over them.

And there shall be one fold, and ONE SHEPHERD.

Jehovah is addressed as THE ROCK in Psalm 18:2;

The Lord is my ROCK...MY GOD....

And we find in 1 Corinthians 10:4 that Jesus shares this title;

....That spiritual ROCK...and that ROCK WAS CHRIST.

Further, the Bible calls both Jesus and Jehovah the following:

Lord of Lords – Deuteronomy 10:17; Revelation 17:14

Holy One – Isaiah 12:6; Acts 3:14, and

King – Psalm 29:10; Revelation 17:14

The Bible also mentions several acts that are ascribed to both Jehovah and Christ. Among the more notable references we find the ability to....

Control the elements – Psalm 107:29; Matthew 8:27

Exist forever – Psalm 102:25-27; Hebrews 1:10-12

Raise the dead – 1 Samuel 2:6; John 5:21, and

Forgive sin – Jeremiah 31:34; Mark 2:7, 10

Psalm 108:5 and Philippians 2:9 teach that both Jehovah and Jesus are exalted and the Bible also shares two very interesting details which they also shared, namely that BOTH Jehovah and Jesus were valued and sold for thirty pieces of silver and BOTH were "pierced"! (See Zechariah 11:12, 13; Matthew 26:14-16, and Zechariah 12:10; Revelation 1:7).

We have previously noted that the important titles of Alpha and Omega, First and Last and I AM are shared by the Father and Son as well.

11

The Pre-Existence Of Christ

If the previous pages have caused us to conclude that Jesus is in fact Jehovah God, we must also of necessity believe that He has always existed. But does the Bible inculcate this?

This question cannot be handled lightly as it is a primary source of heated polemics with many of the major cults, particularly The Way International which teaches that Jesus existed prior to His physical birth only in the Father's "foreknowledge" [21] and the Jehovah's Witnesses who believe that Christ was once none other than Michael the archangel. [22]

---

21 Jesus Christ is Not God. Victor Paul Wierwille. American Christian Press, New Knoxville, Ohio, 1981, pgs. 30-32.

22 Studies in the Scriptures. Watchtower Bible and Tract Society, Brooklyn, New York,

We have seen that the Bible teaches that Jesus was active at the creation of the worlds (See John 1:3; Colossians 1:16, 17; Hebrews 1:1, 2).

We have also considered Scriptures wherein Jesus Himself indicates that He was with the Father before being born of the virgin almost two thousand years ago (See John 1:1; 6:62; 17:5; 17:24; 1 John 1:2).

We know too that Jesus, when referred to as the Alpha and Omega, is said to be the Lord "which is, AND WHICH WAS, and which is to come" (Revelation 1:8, emphasis mine).

But is there any further evidence? Is there a Scripture which plainly says that Jesus pre-existed? Yes, several.

Although we know that John the Baptist was born before Jesus and consequently was six months older (Luke 1), we find this strange announcement in John's Gospel,

> This is he of whom I (John the Baptist) said, after me cometh a man which is preferred before me: FOR HE WAS BEFORE ME (1:30, brackets and emphasis mine).

What in the world did the Baptist mean? Surely he

was aware that he himself was the older of the two, yet he proclaimed that Jesus was before him. What could he mean indeed, unless he was echoing the teaching of the previously considered Scriptures.

Even more evidence can be found in the Old Testament Book of Micah (5:2),

> But thou, Bethlehem Ephratah, though thou be little among the thousands of Judah, yet out of thee shall he come forth unto me that is to be ruler in Israel; (Jesus) WHOSE GOINGS FORTH HAVE BEEN FROM OLD, FROM EVERLASTING (brackets and emphasis mine).

12
Theophanic Appearances Of Christ In The O.T.

In the Old Testament, mention is made of an august, celestial Personage 'who acts in the name of Jehovah', whose name is used interchangeably with that of Jehovah, and who received divine honor and reverence. The more promi- nent names give (sic) to this heavenly being are 'the Angel', the Angel of Je- hovah', 'the Angel of the Presence (or Face)', and 'the Angel (or Messenger) of the Covenant'. He can be none other than the Jehovah of the Old Testament or the Christ of the New Testament – He who becomes the incarnate Word or Logos. [23]

The most striking Old Testament preparation for Christ's Advent, however, were those wonderful theophanic appearances. These pre-incarnate manifestations of His were designed to prepare the world for Christ's more permanent abode in human flesh. Biblical scholars identify 'The angel of the Lord' – 'The angel of his presence' – 'The angel of the Covenant' .... as Christ, the Son of God, in pre-incarnate manifestation. [24]

Proof that the "Angel of the Lord" is far more than just an angel, is provided by the Scriptures themselves when said angel is clearly identified as Jehovah;

And the angel of the Lord called unto him out of heaven, and said, Abraham, Abraham: and he said, Here am I.

And he said, lay not thine hand upon the lad, neither do thou anything unto him: for now I know that thou fearest God, seeing thou hast not withheld thy son, thine only son FROM ME.

23 Taken from CHRISTIAN THEOLOGY, Systematic and Biblical by Emery H. Bancroft. Grand Rapids, Michigan. Published by Zondervan Publishers, 1976, p. 99. With permission of Baptist Bible College & Seminary.

24 Taken from ALL THE DOCTRINES OF THE BIBLE by Herbert Lockyer. Copyright 1964 by the Zondervan Publishing House. Used by permission. p. 38.

Genesis 22:11, 12

> And the angel of the Lord appeared unto him...

> And the Lord said unto him, Surely I will be with thee...

Judges 6:12, 16

> And the angel of God spake unto me in a dream, saying, Jacob: And I said, Here am I.

> And he said, Lift up thine eyes, and see, all the rams which leap upon the cattle are ringstraked, speckled, and grisled: for I have seen all that Laban doeth unto thee.

I AM THE GOD OF BETHEL....

Genesis 31:11-13. See also Judges 2:1-4 (emphasis in all above Scripture is mine)

The significance of the angel's true identity as Jehovah is immediately recognized when one realizes that, according to Scripture, no man has ever seen the Father (John 6:46). This being the case, the "angel of the Lord", as previously mentioned, could only be the pre-incarnate Christ.

There are other theophanies, not addressed as "the angel", but clearly as a man, which further inculcate not only the pre-existence of Christ, but also the fact that He is Jehovah. Consider the following:

And when Abram was ninety years old and nine, the LORD APPEARED to Abram, and said unto him, I AM THE ALMIGHTY GOD; walk before me, and be thou perfect. Genesis 17:1

And THE LORD APPEARED unto him in the plains of Mamre.... Genesis 18:1

And he dreamed, and behold a ladder set up on the earth, and the top of it reached to heaven: and behold the angels of God ascending and descending on it.

And, behold, THE LORD stood above it, and said, I AM THE LORD GOD of Abraham thy father, and THE GOD of Isaac. Genesis 28:12, 13

And Jacob was left alone; and there wrestled a man with him until the breaking of the day...

And Jacob called the name of the place Peniel: for I HAVE SEEN GOD FACE TO FACE, and my life is preserved. Genesis 32:24, 30

And GOD APPEARED unto Jacob again....

And God said unto him, I AM GOD AL-
MIGHTY.... Genesis 35:9, 11

And Jacob said unto Joseph, GOD ALMIGHTY
APPEARED UNTO ME at Luz in the land of Ca-
naan, and blessed me. Genesis 48:3

And God spake unto Moses, and said unto
him, I AM THE LORD: And I APPEARED
unto Abraham, unto Isaac, and unto Jacob,
by the name of GOD ALMIGHTY, but by my
name JEHOVAH was I not known to them.
Exodus 6:2-3

And the Lord spake unto Moses FACE TO
FACE, as a man speaketh unto his friend....
Exodus 33:11

The LORD talked with you FACE TO FACE
in the mount out of the midst of the fire.
Deuteronomy 5:4

And there arose not a prophet since in Israel like unto Moses, whom the LORD knew
FACE TO FACE. Deuteronomy 34:10

And the angel of the Lord said unto him,
Why askest thou thus after my name, seeing it is secret? And Manoah said unto his

wife, We shall surely die, because WE HAVE SEEN GOD. Judges 13:18, 22

See also 1 Kings 3:5; 9:2; 11:9; 2 Chronicles 1:7; etc. (emphasis in all above Scripture is mine)

Lest the reader find himself uncomfortable with the conclusion that the angel of the Lord is actually the pre-incarnate Christ, the following is offered as absolute proof of the doctrine:

> And the ANGEL OF GOD, which went before the camp of Israel, removed AND WENT BEHIND THEM.... Exodus 14:19

Compared with:

> Moreover, brethren, I would not that ye should be ignorant, how that all our fathers were under the cloud, and all passed through the sea;
>
> And were all baptized unto Moses in the cloud and in the sea;
>
> And did all eat the same spiritual meat;
>
> And did all drink the same spiritual drink: for they drank of that spiritual Rock THAT FOLLOWED THEM: AND THAT ROCK WAS CHRIST. 1 Corinthians 10:1-4

So we see that the Bible itself declares that the "angel of the Lord" was in fact Christ.

Obviously, the cults which promulgate the erroneous theory that Jesus did not physically exist before His birth in Bethlehem are ignoring a powerful testimony to the contrary, namely Hebrews 13:8, "Jesus Christ THE SAME yesterday, and today, and for ever" (emphasis mine).

13

Every Knee Shall Bow...
To Whom?

Most every Christian is familiar with the wonderful declaration of Philippians 2:10 & 11....

> That at the name of Jesus every knee should bow, of things in heaven, and things in earth, and things under the earth;

> And that every tongue should confess that Jesus Christ is Lord, to the glory of God the Father.

Not many however, are aware that this passage is actually a direct quote from the Old Testament Book of Isaiah. The only difference, and it is a major one, is that in the O.T. It is Jehovah Himself uttering the prophecy and He claims that every knee will bow TO HIM and every tongue will confess TO HIM....

> I (Jehovah) have sworn by myself, the word is gone out of my mouth in righteousness, and shall not return, that UNTO ME every knee shall bow, every tongue shall swear.... 45:23 (brackets & emphasis mine)

How can the same reference, the same prophecy, the same declaration be applied to BOTH Jesus and Jehovah...unless of course Jesus IS Jehovah!

In this instance the Watchtower has actually proven quite helpful to the Christian position on the deity of Christ by stating in the introduction to their Kingdom Interlinear Translation (p. 18) that the modern-day translator must determine where the New Testament writers have quoted from the Old Testament and then refer back to the O.T. Passage in question to discover whether the divine name was used.

When this methodology is implemented in the aforementioned passage, we discover that Philippians 2:10, 11 is actually declaring that Jesus is Jehovah!

A paraphrase of the passage could be properly

rendered, "...Every tongue shall confess that Jesus Christ is Jehovah to the glory of God the Father".

To this logic of the Watchtower we wholeheartedly say, amen.

GOD WITH US

One final Scripture reference which supports the deity of the Lord Jesus is found in the Gospel of Matthew,

> Behold, a virgin shall be with child, and shall bring forth a son, and they shall call his name Emmanuel, which being inter- preted is, GOD WITH US. 1:23 (emphasis mine)

Truly this verse sums up the preceding pages quite adequately. When Jesus was "with us" here on earth, God was with us.

That this is more than simply a spiritual or alle- gorical statement is obvious when it is considered alongside passages already considered (John 1:1- 3, 14; 1 Timothy 3:16; Colossians 2:9; etc).

Having offered ample proof for the deity of the Lord Jesus, we shall close this section by considering one of the most troublesome areas for those who attempt to present said deity to a cultist.

14
Humanity vs. Deity

Perhaps the most effective method of detracting from the deity of Jesus is by magnifying His humanity.

The Jehovah's Witnesses make constant use of this deceptive manipulation of the Scriptures by presenting the un-informed with a barrage of "proof texts" which stress the human qualities and/or characteristics of Jesus (e.g., Matthew 8:24; 21:18; John 19:28; etc). This approach is then intensified by pointing out passages which appear to indicate a definite distinction between Christ and Jehovah (e.g., John 14:28; etc).

This practice of using only some of the Scriptural references relating to a paricular doctrine or subject rather than ALL of the applicable passages is known as selective biblicity.

That the Word of God surely teaches the humanity of Jesus is not at all questioned by the Christian Church. The question which does appear at this particular juncture however, is whether or not said humanity in any way detracts from His divinity.

Before proceeding further, let us first confirm that the Bible does indeed inculcate the humanity of the Lord.

First of all, we note that the Lord, while here on earth, was in possession of a spirit, soul and body. Dr. Emery H. Bancroft states:

> When Jesus Christ became incarnate, He came into possession of a real human, physical nature and was "made in the likeness of men." This human nature, however, was not a carnal nature. It was sinless.

1. He possessed a physical body: "For in that she hath poured this ointment on my body, she did it for my burial" (Matt. 26:12).

2. He possessed a rational soul: "Then saith he unto them, My soul is exceeding sorrowful, even unto death: tarry ye here, and watch with me" (Matt. 26:38).

3. He possessed a human spirit: "And when Jesus had cried with a loud voice, he said, Father, into thy hands I commend my spirit: and having said thus, he gave up the ghost" (Luke 23:46). The denial of Christ's true physical nature is a mark of the spirit of antichrist (1 John 4:2, 3). [25]

Additional support for this reasoning is superabundant within Scripture and is readily evidenced by Jesus' frequent displays of human characteristics. We read of Him showing sorrow, hunger, anger, fatigue and thirst (John 11:35; Matthew 4:2; Mark 3:5; Matthew 8:24; John 19:28).

Another aspect of Jesus' humanity is evidenced by His human parentage. Of course we know that He was miraculously conceived in the womb of the virgin. However, as we shall see, He was, nonetheless, subject to a normal human infancy and upbringing.

The Scriptures clearly speak of this human parentage (Matthew 1:18; 2:11; 12:47; 13:55 John 2:1; Romans 1:3; Galatians 4:4; etc).

As previously alluded to, the infancy and development of Jesus was also comparable to that of any other human boy. We find that He was subject to the basic laws of human development in that He

25 Taken from ELEMENTAL THEOLOGY by Emery H. Bancroft. Published by Zondervan Publishers, Grand Rapids, Michigan, 1977. pgs. 133-34. With permission of Baptist Bible College & Seminary.

grew in both wisdom and stature, learned obedience, suffered temptation, and was made perfect
through sufferings (Luke 2:40, 46-49, 52; Hebrews
2:10, 18; 5:8).

Once again referring to Bancroft, we learn that Jesus was indeed human to the extent of possessing
spiritual limitations....

> In the incarnation, Jesus Christ exchanged
> His independent life for the dependent life;
> His sovereignty for subordination; living
> His life as a man. He limited Himself to the
> means and methods by which divine power
> is obtained and exercised by man.

a. Jesus Christ was dependent upon prayer for
power: "And in the morning, rising up a great
while before day, he went out, and departed into
a solitary place, and there he prayed" (Mark
1:35-cf. Luke 22:41-45; John 6:15; Heb. 5:7).
In the Scriptures we have mention of twenty-five
times that Jesus prayed. He obtained power for
work and for moral victory as other men do, by
prayer. He was subject to human conditions for
obtaining what He desired.

b. Christ was dependent for power upon the anoint-
ing Spirit: "How God anointed Jesus of Nazareth with the Holy Ghost and with power: who
went about doing good, and healing all that

were oppressed of the devil; for God was with him" (Acts 10:38). The period of Christ's dependency was the period of His humiliation. It extended from Bethlehem to Olivet, or during the period of His incarnate life upon earth. He then resumed the glory which He had with the Father before the world was, and all the prerogatives of His godhood. [26]

Let it also be understood that the man Jesus was also limited on an intellectual level.

We have already seen that He was able to learn (Luke 2:52). Furthermore, He was able to obtain knowledge by simple observation (Mark 11:13) and, He was not omniscient (Mark 13:32). (However, in reference to this last statement it should be pointed out that Jesus did, on occasion, display characteristics of omniscience and omnipresence e.g. John 1:47-50).

In the light of the ample evidence provided for the deity of the Lord Jesus it is necessary to find a suitable explanation for the many references which clearly refer to His humanity.

It is of the utmost importance that we do not make the error of rejecting His deity because of His humanity or vice-versa.

26 Taken from ELEMENTAL THEOLOGY, by Emery H. Bancroft. Published by Zondervan Publishers, Grand Rapids, Michigan, 1977. pgs. 136-7. With permission of Baptist Bible College & Seminary.

As mentioned earlier, this is precisely the error of the Watchtower.

Jehovah's Witnesses, and others who share their beliefs, must be brought to the place where they are willing to accept all that the Bible has to say rather than simply hinging their entire belief system on "proof texts" which are generally taken out of context to begin with.

As stated, the Christian Church does not have a problem with the humanity of the Lord Jesus. We accept it, believe it, preach it and teach it. However, we also accept and believe the previously considered passages which undeniably teach that Jesus truly is God in human form.

THE KENOSIS THEORY

The explanation of the merging deity and humanity of Jesus can be found in the so-called Kenosis passage (Philippians 2:5-8). We shall quote at length a valuable summation of said theory:

> 'Let this mind be in you, which was also in Christ Jesus: Who, being in the form of God, thought it not robbery to be equal with God: but made himself of no reputation, and took upon him the form of a servant, and was made in the likeness of men: and being

found in fashion as a man, he humbled himself, and became obedient unto death, even the death of the cross' (Phil. 2:5-8).

The self-emptying (kenosis) of Christ, which was a voluntary act, consisted of the surrender of the independent exercise of the divine attributes. To illustrate, finite beings have the power to a certain degree to restrict the limits of consciousness. By acts of the will, we may exclude many things from our minds. We make an effort to forget, and in a measure we suceed. This is a feeble illustration, but it gives us a faint clue of the possibilities of self-renunciation on the part of the Son of God. How the independent exercise of the divine attributes could be surrendered, even for a time, would be inconceivable if we were regarding the Logos, or Word, as He is in Himself, seated upon the throne of the universe. The matter is somewhat easier when we remember that it was not the Logos as such, but rather the God-man, Jesus Christ, in whom the Logos submitted to this humiliation and thus made self-limitation possible.

It was the union of the human and divine that limited the Logos. The general sense is that He divested Himself of the peculiar mode of existence which was proper and peculiar to Him as one with God. He laid aside the form of God. But in so doing, He did not divest Himself of His divine nature. The change was a change of state: the form of a servant for the form of God. His personality continued the same. His self-emptying was not self-extinction, nor was the divine Being changed into a mere man. In His humanity He retained the consciousness of deity, and in His incarnate state He retained the mind that animated Him before His incarnation. He was not able to assert equality, be He was able not to assert it. Thus, without trying to explain away its force, we may accept the inspired declaration that Christ truly emptied Himself.

In the Philippians passage quoted above, we read, 'Thought it not robbery'; that is, He viewed His possession of the fullness of the eternal nature as securely and inalienably His own. And so 'emptied Himself,' or so made Himself void of His own account. So sure was Christ of His claim to deity that without hesitation He could empty Himself of the outward manifestation of His deity and the independent exercise of His attributes.

The purpose of the self-emptying and incarnation was redemptive. Deity in the distinctive sense could become incarnate in human form because human personality contains the essential elements of all personality: self-consciousness, intelligence, feeling, moral nature, and will. Personality is the point at which creation in the ascent returns to God. Man bears the divine image. The self-emptying of Christ in the Incarnation was the voluntary suspension of the full exercise of divine attributes, though potentially all divine resources were present. [27]

It is essential that we grasp the paramount fact that Jesus most assuredly did not completely relinquish His deity in the incarnation. He did not become "fully man" to the total exclusion of His Godhood. Nor did He retain His divinity to the complete exclusion of humanity. And yet, by the same token, He was not half-God and half-man. Truly the most accurate way to present the matter is by saying that Jesus was FULLY God and FULLY man when He walked the earth two thousand years ago.

It is difficult to determine which of the two would be the greater error; the denial of Jesus' deity or that of His humanity, for truly both aspects are equally important. The incarnation was quite necessary....

The union of two natures in one person is necessary to constitute Jesus Christ as a proper mediator between man and God. His twofold nature gives Him fellowship with

27 Taken from ELEMENTAL THEOLOGY, by Emery H. Bancroft. Published by Zondervan Publishers, Grand Rapids, Michigan, 1977. pgs. 147-8. With permission of Baptist Bible College & Seminary.

both parties, since it involves an equal dignity with God and at the same time a perfect sympathy with man (Hebrews 2:17, 18; 4:15, 16). This twofold nature, moreover, enables Him to present to both God and man proper terms of reconciliation. Being man, He can make atonement for man; being God, His atonement has infinite value, while both His deity and humanity combine to move the hearts of offenders and constrain them to submission and love (1 Timothy 2:5; Hebrews 7:25). [28]

As mentioned above, it was necessary for Jesus to partake of humanity in order to have "a perfect sympathy with man". We should take great comfort in the knowledge that the Lord truly understands the hardships and struggles we endure. Many times as caring people we attempt to calm an upset friend or loved one with the common phrase, "I know what you must be going through". Unfortunately, this is often uttered even when it is completely untrue. Not so with Jesus. He truly does understand our trials, struggles and hardships because He partook of the same.

Many feel that this also illustrates another reason for the incarnation – Namely, that no one will be able to criticize the Lord for unfairness at the Judg-

28 Taken from CHRISTIAN THEOLOGY, Systematic and Biblical, by Emery H. Bancroft. Published by Zondervan Publishers, Grand Rapids, Michigan, 1976. p. 108. With permission of Baptist Bible College & Seminary.

ment Seat with the accusation that He "Just doesn't know what I've been through" or "He can't possibly understand just how difficult it is to be human".

It is my sincere hope that the reader has been provided with sufficient information to support his/her belief in both the deity and humanity of the Lord Jesus Christ.

In the following section we shall examine several of the "Scriptural" arguments presented against the deity of Jesus.

15

Scripture Twisting

A RESPONSE TO THE ASSERTIONS OF THE CULTS

It should come as no surprise that in their attempt to disprove the deity of the Lord Jesus, the cults have found it necessary to develop their own peculiar interpretations of several key Scripture passages.

It is the purpose of this chapter to consider several of these misleading interpretations and assertions which are set forth by the various cults and isms of the day in order to determine whether or not their arguments are valid.

However, we shall limit ourselves to several of the arguments which are set forth by the Watchtower organization as they have gone to great lengths to develop many scholarly-sounding points which truly deserve responses.

IS JESUS ONLY "A" GOD?

As we have already seen, the Jehovah's Witnesses teach that John 1:1 should read, "...the Word was a god".

We have shown the incompatibility of this errone-ous interpretation with other passages which clear-ly proclaim that there is but one true God (thereby making Jesus a false god if the Watchtower's trans-lation is used).

However, since this passage is a major source of argumentation with the Witnesses, I feel that ad-ditional evidence against their position should be offered, hence, the following:

> This text 'THE WORD WAS A GOD' has been a problem for four presidents of Je-hovah's Witnesses. C.T. Russell thought he found relief when in 1876 N.H. Barbour, an Adventist, introduced him to Wilson's EM-PHATIC DIAGLOTT. Mr Wilson never studied Biblical Greek in a college. He was a fol-lower of John Thomas, a 'false prophet' and founder of the Christadelphians. Thomas nor

Wilson believed 'THE WORD WAS GOD'. In the interlinear feature of his book which is no translation at all, Wilson placed 'a god' under theos. In his translation however, of theos, he wrote: 'the LOGOS was God.'

F.W. Franz, the current president of the Jehovah's Witnesses, realized the deficiency of the DIAGLOTT, decided to translate his own Bible called THE NEW WORLD TRANSLATION OF THE HOLY SCRIPTURES. Mr. Franz never studied biblical or koine Greek. He did not graduate from any college nor did he receive a Rhodes Scholarship as he claims. He translates the phrase 'the Word was a god.' in his KINGDOM INTERLINEAR he interlineates 'god was the Word.' Such a translation creates another god. 'To us there is one God.'

F.W. Franz found a translation that agrees with his, THE NEW TESTAMENT by Johannes Greber. (SEE MAKE SURE OF ALL THINGS p. 489 1965 revision). Who was Johannes Greber? He is the author of another book: COMMUNICATION WITH THE SPIRIT WORLD OF GOD. In it Greber writes on page 300:

> 'After I had convinced myself at the spiritistic meetings that God's spirits speak to

men through mediums, as they had spoken to the early Christian communities, my first thought was to beg for full enlightenment on these problems concerning Christ. Who was Christ? My request was granted, to the smallest details, and that knowledge thenceforth constituted the most precious possession of my soul. What follows, I shall repeat the truths regarding Christ. His life, and his work of Redemption, as they were imparted to me by the spirit which taught them.' The spirit said: 'At that time you were told that Christ is the highest of the spirits created by God and the sole one to be created directly; Christ Himself was not God, but only the first of God's sons,'

It is interesting that this is exactly what Franz the president of Jehovah's Witnesses teaches. Franz claims to get information from angels also. The Apostle John warns:

'Beloved, do not believe every spirit, but test the spirits to see whether they are of God; for many false prophets have gone out into the world' 1 John 4:1.

Greber's translation is directly from the demon world. He is quoted in

Watchtower publications. (See AID TO BIBLE UNDERSTANDING p. 1134) In the Watchtower publication ALL SCRIPTURE IS INSPIRED OF GOD & BENEFICIAL p. 327 it states:

'Note what Hebrew and Greek scholar Alexander Thomson has to say in his review of the NEW WORLD TRANSLATION: ' The translation is evidently the work of skilled and clever scholars,' THE DIFFERENTIATOR, April 1952. This sentence is another Watchtower lie. The late Mr. Alexander Thomson was not a Greek or Hebrew Scholar. He in fact did not even formally study Greek or Hebrew in any school according to his co-editor Dr. Frank Neil Pohorlak of Inglewood, CA. Mr. Thomson was employed in a bank in Scotland and did not believe that Jesus was God.

WHAT DO GREEK SCHOLARS THINK ABOUT JEHOVAH'S WITNESSES TRANSLATION OF JOHN 1:1?

Dr. Julius R. Mantey: calls the Watchtower translation of John 1:1 'A GROSSLY MISLEADING TRANSLATION.'

It is neither scholarly nor reasonable to translate John 1:1 'the Word was a god.' But of all the scholars in the world, so far as we know, none have translated this verse as Jehovah's Witnesses have done.' Bruce M. Metzger, Professor of New Testament Language and Literature at Princeton Theological Seminary said: 'Far more pernicious in this same verse is the rendering...'and the Word was a god'. It must be stated quite frankly that, if the Jehovah's Witnesses take this translation seriously, they are polytheists. In view of the additional light which is available during this age of Grace, such a representation is even more reprehensible then were the heathenish, polytheistic errors into which ancient Israel was so prone to fall. As a matter of solid fact, however, such a rendering is a frightful mistranslation.'

Dr. J.J. Griesback:

'So numerous and clear are the arguments and testimonies of Scriptures in favor of the true Deity of Christ, that I can hardly imagine how, upon the admission of the Divine authority of Scripture, and with regard to fair rules of interpretation, this doctrine can by any man be called in doubt. Especially the passage John 1:1 is so clear and so superior to all exception, that by no daring efforts of either commentators or critics can it be snatched out of the hands of the defenders of the truth.'

Dr. Eugene A. Nida (Head of the Translation Department of the American Bible Society Translators of the GOOD NEWS BIBLE):

'With regard to John 1:1 there is, of course, a complication simply because the NEW WORLD TRANSLATION was apparently done by persons who did not take seriously the syntax of the Greek'.

Dr. William Barclay (University of Glasgow, Scotland):

'The deliberate distortion of truth by this sect is seen in their New Testament translations. John 1:1 is translated: '...the Word was a god', a translation which is grammatically impossible. It is abundantly clear that a sect which can translate the New Testament like that is intellectually dishonest.' THE EXPOSITORY TIMES Nov. 1953

Dr. B.F. Westcott (Whose Greek text is used in JW KINGDOM INTERLINEAR):

'The predicate (God) stands emphatically first, as in 4:24. It is necessarily without the article...No idea of inferiority of nature is suggested by the form of expression, which simply affirms the true Deity of the Word... In the third clause 'the Word' is declared to be 'God' and so included in the unity of the Godhead.' Dr. Ernest C. Colwell (University of Chicago): 'A definite predicate nominative has the article when it follows a verb; it does not have the article when it precedes the verb;...this statement cannot be regarded as strange in the prologue of the gospel which reaches its climax in the confession of Thomas. 'My Lord and my God.' John 20:28

Dr. F.F. Bruce (University of Manchester, England):

'Much is made by Arian amateur grammarians of the omission of the definite article with 'God' in the phrase 'And the Word was God'. Such an omission is common with nouns in a predicate construction. 'a god' would be totally indefensible.'

Dr. Paul L. Kaufman (Portland, OR.):

'The Jehovah's Witness people evidence an abysmal ignorance of the basic tenets of Greek grammar in their mistranslation of John 1:1.'

Dr. Charles L. Feinberg (La Mirada, CA.):

'I can assure you that the rendering which the Jehovah's Witnesses give John 1:1 is not held by any reputable Greek scholar.'

Dr. Harry A. Sturz:

(Dr. Sturz is Chairman of the Language Department and Professor of Greek at Biola College): 'Therefore, the NWT rendering: 'the Word was a god' is not a 'literal' but an ungrammatical and tendential translation. A literal translation in English can be nothing other than: 'the Word was God.'

THE BIBLE COLLECTOR July-December, 1971 p. 12. [29]

---

29 Taken from QUESTIONS FOR JEHOVAH'S WITNESSES WHO LOVE THE TRUTH by Bill Cetnar. Kunkletown, PA. 1983 p. 55

16
Was Jesus Created?

The Witnesses assert that several passages of Scripture indicate that Jesus was created and, they say, if this is the case He simply cannot be God since God has always existed.

Let's give credit where credit is due...There really is a passage or two which, on the surface, appear to support their theory. However, "on the surface" is not good enough when one is referring to the Word of God. We must be very careful to be sure we are fully understanding what each verse is really saying. We shall now examine the references in question.

Who (Jesus) is the image of the invisible

> God, the FIRSTBORN of every creature...
> Colossians 1:15 (brackets & emphasis
> mine)

The Witnesses assert that because Jesus is referred to as "the firstborn of every creature", He must have been, "the first one born". Consequently, if He was the first one born, He cannot be Jehovah.

This explanation sounds reasonable enough and it is easy to see how simple it would be to nod our heads in agreement while saying, "You just may have something there". However, let's take the time to take a closer look at the passage to see if the Witnesses have indeed found its true meaning.

We begin with a rather foolish sounding question, "Does FIRSTBORN always mean the first one born?" The answer to this question will prove interesting in this case.

While keeping the above verse in mind I encourage you to consider Genesis 41:51, 52...

> And Joseph called the name of THE FIRST-BORN MANASSEH...

> And the name of THE SECOND called he EPHRAIM... (emphasis mine)

There should be no question about these verses. They are clear and concise in what they offer: Manasseh was FIRSTBORN, Ephraim was SECOND. What could be easier?

But, before patting the Watchtower on the back I suggest that we consider one more passage which is sure to add an interesting "twist":

> They shall come with weeping, and with supplications will I lead them: I will cause them to walk by the rivers of waters in a straight way, wherein they shall not stumble: for I am a father to Israel, and EPHRAIM IS MY FIRSTBORN. Jeremiah 31:9 (emphasis mine)

The JW assertion of Jesus necessarily being the "first one born" is hereby eradicated.

The reader may ask how one Scripture can call Manasseh the firstborn while another refers to Ephraim as firstborn. The answer to this logical query is actually the crux of the issue.

Without excessive detail and wordiness, a simple response should suffice to answer this question. Said rather basically, in Hebrew chronology, firstborn (prototokos) often meant "preeminent". Careful study of the Scriptures will show that Manasseh did in deed hold the position of FIRSTBORN until, through sin, he forfeited the position. Ephraim was then "promoted" as it were, to preeminence.

When considered in this light the entire context and message of the following verses (Colossians 1:16-18) becomes increasingly informative since we read of Jesus having PREEMINENCE in all things (v. 18)!

Let it be further stated that if Paul had in fact meant to imply that Jesus was the first one created, as the Watchtower asserts, he would have no doubt used the Greek word PROTOKTISIS which means "first created".

This reasoning may be taken further still by considering the use of the word "firstborn" in Colossians 1:18 where Jesus is referred to as the FIRSTBORN from the dead.

Was Jesus really the firstborn from the dead?

No, He wasn't. At least not if the word FIRSTBORN is taken to mean the "first one". The Scriptures are replete with accounts of people being raised from the dead BEFORE Jesus was (2 Kings 4:32-35; 13:20, 21; Mark 5:35-43; Luke 7:11-17; John 11:43-45).

However, Jesus certainly was the PREEMINENT one to be raised from the dead since He came forth in a glorified body of flesh and bone never to die again!

DID JESUS HAVE A BEGINNING?

The verse in question is Revelation 3:14...

> And unto the angel of the church of the Laodiceans write; These things saith the Amen (Jesus), the faithful and true witness, THE BEGINNING OF THE CREATION OF GOD; (brackets & emphasis mine)

The Watchtower reason for this argument is similar to that of the previously considered example — If Jesus "had a beginning" He could not be Jehovah since Jehovah has always existed.

Once again, we admit, the reasoning, though faulty, does pose a worthwhile question.

Did Jesus have a beginning?

To respond to this question we must first ascertain whether or not the verse is even suggesting that He did. The Greek word which is translated "beginning" in this verse (arche) is more properly rendered as "origin" or "source". The JW's are not at liberty to argue this fact since in the 1950 edition of their New World Translation they used the word

ORIGINALLY in the place of BEGINNING in John 1:1.

We have already noted that Jesus is unmistakably set forth as the Creator (John 1:1-3; Colossians 1:16) and this verse (Revelation 3:14) actually serves to strengthen this position!

Hence when properly rendered we find that Jesus is in fact the origin and/or source of creation!

17

The Father Is
Greater Than Jesus

This statement of John 14:28, uttered by Jesus Himself, receives no argument from the Christian Church. When Jesus humbled Himself and took the form of a slave (Philippians 2:5-8) the Father was certainly positionally greater than Jesus.

The reader will note, however, that the text does not read, "The Father is BETTER than Jesus". If Jesus had said "better" rather than "greater", the Jehovah's Witnesses position would be correct. No question.

But Jesus did not say "better".

I appreciate the manner in which Dr. Walter R.

Martin illustrates this situation by comparing the President of the United States to the citizens of the United States.

Positionally, as Dr. Martin explains, the President is greater than any of the citizens. However, the President would be the last person to ever say that he is "better" than any other citizen!

Jesus' declaration of John 14:28 in no way diminishes His deity.

WISDOM BROUGHT FORTH – PROVERBS 8:22-24

Due to the fact that Jesus is referred to as "the power and wisdom of God" in 1 Corinthians, the Jehovah's Witnesses feel that He (Christ) must have been created by Jehovah since Proverbs 8 indicates that wisdom was in deed brought forth or created. However, two basic points quickly dismantle this inaccurate use of cross-reference.

First of all, if the Watchtower is correct in this assumption we must admit that there was a time when Jehovah was completely without power and wisdom! This is, of course, unthinkable.

Secondly, consideration of Proverbs 8:1-3 and 9:1-4 will show that "wisdom" is spoken of in the female gender!

Frankly, Christ is not even mentioned in Proverbs 8 and the burden of proof is upon those (JW's) who say that He is.

HEAD OF CHRIST IS GOD – 1 CORINTHIANS 11:3

An excellent explanation of this passage is offered by F.W.Thomas in the book Masters of Deception. I quote...

> "But I would have you know, that the head of every man is Christ; and the head of the woman is the man; and the head of Christ is God" (1 Cor. 11:3).

> "The JW's use this text to show that the Son is subject to the Father. We readily agree that the mediatorial Son is indeed subject to the Father. However, the subjection of the Son to the Father does not necessitate a rejection of the Trinity. Quite the contrary, for within the Godhead there exists the Divine priniciple of subjection and equality. What we mean is that the Son is both subject to the Father and yet equal with the Father. This is not a contradiction. Rather it is an expression of the highest kind of love when two equals voluntarily submit themselves to each other. Not only is the Son subject to the Father, but the Father also

submits Himself to the Son. None can argue against the scriptural fact that the Father is committed to fulfill the wishes and desires of the Son (John 16:23). Likewise the Son is also committed to fulfill the will of the Father. Our text at 1 Corinthians 11:3 speaks of a husband and wife relationship. This scripture further suggests that a similar unity exists between the Father and Son. Upon examining this text we find that a woman is in subjection to her husband. However, does this mean that because a woman is in subjection to her husband that she is less of a human being than her husband? We know that even though the woman is subject to the man, she is still of the same essence and substance as the man. In other words, the woman is equal in substance to the man and is as much of a human being as her husband despite her subjection. The point here is that the woman is only positionally inferior to the man.

"While we are on this theme, let us consider the scripture which speaks of Christ being subject for a time to Mary and Joseph. We read where Jesus "went down with them and came to Nazareth and was subject unto them" (Luke 2:51). Does this mean that Jesus was less than Mary and Joseph? Certainly such could not be the case. It is clear that Jesus was only "positionally inferior" to His earthly parents for a time. This same principle applies in Christ's relationship with the Father. Even though the Son is subject to the Father, He is still of the same essence of the Father. It was Christ Himself who declared, "I and my Father are one" (John 10:30). Since the Son is of the same essence as the Father, the Son is therefore eternal and most certainly cannot be a creature as the JW's falsely teach.

"The Bible tells us that Christ Jesus is the "one mediator between God and men" (1 Tim. 2:5). We gather from this text, as well as 1 Cor. 15:24, that the subjection of the Son to the Father is only temporary; it will last only as long as Christ acts as mediator between God and men. When the Son ultimately puts down all rule and all authority and all power, He then delivers up the kingdom to the Father. When this takes place the mediatorial office of Christ comes to an end. The Son then resumes His former position of equality and glory which He shared with the Father before the worlds were made (John 17:5). The problem with the JW's is that they stress the scriptures which speak of the humiliation of Christ, but ignore the texts which speak of His equality with the Father. Thus they get a distorted view of the magnificence of Christ. [30]

---

30 Taken from MASTERS OF DECEPTION by F. W. Thomas. Published by Baker Book House, Grand Rapids, Michigan, 1985, pgs. 19-20. Used by permission.

NO MAN HAS SEEN GOD – JOHN 1:18

This passage is perhaps the most efficacious of all Watchtower tactics to discredit the deity of Jesus. It is particularly powerful when used against non-or new Christians who simply cannot argue with the straightforwardness of the passage...No man has seen God, therefore, how can Jesus be God since men most certainly saw Him (Jesus)?

A fair question.

This question cannot be handled lightly. It poses a serious contradiction, albeit only superficially, which has the potential of shattering the orthodox position on the deity of Jesus in the mind of the babe in Christ.

Please allow me the luxury of setting forth the explanation to this situation in a rather simplistic fashion which I will follow-up with a more in-depth response.

Quite simply, when the Scriptures declare that "no man has seen God", it is the responsibility of the student to carefully consider the context of the passage in which the statement is found. For example, is the declaration referring specifically to the Father (which is clearly the case in John 6:46), or perhaps to all three members of the Trinity?

As we learned in the preceding section, the O.T. Is replete with references to men actually seeing Jehovah (Genesis 17:1; 18:1; 32:24, 30; 35:9, 11; 48:3; Exodus 6:2-3; 33:11; Deuteronomy 5:4; 34:10, etc.). It is our position that it was actually the pre-incarnate Christ who appeared in these passages and is identified as Jehovah (Colossians 2:9).

While keeping this in mind, consider the following statement which is commonly uttered by Jehovah's Witnesses when discussing the deity of our Lord:

> "Moses wasn't even allowed to see Jehovah! He had to be set in the clift of a rock and was only permitted to see Jehovah's back! Obviously, no one can see Jehovah!"

It does sound convincing, doesn't it? After all, the Witnesses do have a valid point...Or do they?

This argument of the Watchtower makes use of a very misleading tactic which epitomizes the phrase "Scripture twisting".

The problem is that most people, yes even believers, will quickly nod their head in agreement and admit that they do remember reading that in their own Bible.

But let's take the time to cautiously consider what the passage in question really says.

Exodus 33:11 finds the Lord speaking with Moses FACE TO FACE. It can't be made much clearer than that can it? What else could the words "face to face" possibly mean if not that they were looking directly at one another? However, just in case that wasn't clear enough for us, the Holy Spirit added, "as a man speaketh unto his friend".

Just how does a man speak to his friend? Is one of them invisible while the other speaks to him? Is one hundreds of miles away from the other using some form of telepathy or thought-transference to communicate? Of course not. When a man speaks to a friend, other than via the telephone naturally, the two are together, looking at one another. Therefore the message of the aforementioned Scripture is undeniable. Moses was looking directly at Jehovah while the two talked with one another.

Now then, back to the argument of the Watchtower. I offer you the key to understanding the entire situation. It is found in verse 18:

> And he (Moses) said, I beseech thee, SHEW ME THY GLORY...(brackets & emphasis mine)

By simply suggesting that Moses' request to see Jehovah was denied, the Watchtower causes the average person to agree that "no man can see God". However, as is made clear in verse eleven, Moses could already see Him! He was standing with Him, conversing with Him. The bottom line is that Moses DID NOT ask to see God...Why would he ask to see Someone he could already see? The truth is that Moses asked to see Jehovah's glory. This request was denied simply because a mortal man in a mortal body truly cannot see the glory of God and survive!

This account should display the extreme importance of attention to each and every word of a Scripture passage!

Let us now return to the initial question – Can God be seen by man?

Perhaps it would be easier to re-phrase the question as in the following:

Q. Can any man see the Father?
A. No. Scipture is clear on this (John 6:46).

Q. Can any man see the Holy Spirit?
A. No. The Holy Spirit does not have a physical form and therefore cannot be seen other than in special circumstance (i.e., when He took on the form of a dove at Jesus' baptism – Matthew 3:16).

Q. Can God be seen in all of His glory?
A. No. The previously considered passage from the Book of Exodus makes this abundantly clear.

Q. Can God be seen at all?

A. Yes. Paul declares that Jehovah can indeed be seen, in His fullness, in the Person of Jesus Christ (Colossians 2:9). This teaching is further promulgated when Jesus' words to Philip are considered, "He that hath seen me hath seen the Father..." (John 14:9). More modern translations of the Bible sum this teaching up quite well by stating, "For in Him (Jesus) ALL THE FULLNESS OF DEITY DWELLS IN BODILY FORM" (Colossians 2:9 NASV brackets & emphasis mine).

Consider it this way: We cannot see our soul. We cannot see our spirit. But we can see our body and our body is the physical expression of all three.

Similarly, we cannot see the Father. We cannot see the Holy Spirit. But we can see Jesus and Jesus, according to Scripture, is the physical expression of all three members of the Godhead! To deny this would require the total rejection of literally dozens of O.T. Passages, already considered and discussed, unhesitatingly state that God was seen by men and women. which IS JESUS A CREATURE? One of the most glaring and unscriptural attempts of the Watchtower to refute the deity of the Lord Jesus can be seen in their atrocious rendering of Colossians 1:15-17....

> He is the image of the invisible God, the firstborn of all creation, because by means of him all (other) things were created in the heavens and upon the earth...All (other) things have been created through him and for him. Also, he is before all (other) things and by means of him all (other) things were made to exist. New World Translation -Brackets in the original

It is difficult to be civil when discussing this blatant and diabolical mis-translation of the Word of God. In case the reader hasn't yet noticed, allow me to point out that the Watchtower has purposely and conveniently added the word "other" into the text in question four times. This was necessary in order for them to distort the clear-cut announcement of the passage that Jesus is the Creator and therefore He is Jehovah.

Consider a more reliable translation of the verse:

> For by Him all things were created, both in the heavens and on earth, visible and invisible, whether thrones or dominions or rulers or authorities – all things have been created by Him and for Him. New American Standard Version

Notice how the simple insertion of the word "other" totally changes the meaning and message of the text. According to the NWT, Jesus is one of the "things" created! Blasphemous to say the least. According to scholarly translations, Jesus is not a mere "created thing", He is none other than Jehovah God the Creator! Quite a difference. Little wonder the Watchtower saw the need to sabotage the true meaning of the text!

It should also be noted that the word "other" does not appear in any of the original texts or early Greek manuscripts. It would be good for the Witnesses to heed the warning of Revelation 22:18, 19!

The Jehovah's Witnesses, in a feeble attempt to excuse this horrific alteration of God's Word, will liken the use of the word "other", encased in brackets, to the italicized words of the King James Version. However, there is no comparison since the italicized words are inserted only for the sake of clarity in translating to English from the original languages and they in no way change or alter the meaning or message of the passages in which they are found.

Actually, I have found that when discussing this passage, and the New World Translation adaptation of it, with Jehovah's Witnesses, most will not bring themselves to refer to Jesus as a "thing" even though this is what their Bible teaches!

CHRIST IN SUBJECTION...

And when all things shall be subdued unto him, then shall the Son also himself be subject unto him that put all things under him, that God may be all in all. 1 Corinthians 15:28

The verse above is a favorite of the Watchtower Bible and Tract Society. This text, they say, proves that Jesus is not equal with Jehovah since He (Jesus) is in subjection to Him.

Once again, at first glance, the Witnesses seem to present a valid argument against the deity of Jesus. However, a simple comparison of the verse below serves to succinctly shatter this approach as well...

And he (Jesus) went down with them (Mary and Joseph), and came to Nazareth, and was subject unto them... Luke 2:51 (brackets mine)

If the J.W. approach for interpreting 1 Corinthians 15:28 is used when interpreting the verse above (and it would have to be since the same word, "subject", appears in both verses), we would have to accept that Jesus, the Son of God, the Messiah, the King, was inferior to Mary and Joseph!

Of course this argument is preposterous! The fact

that Jesus was in subjection to His earthly parents denotes, as briefly touched on earlier, an attitude of loving obedience, NOT inferiority.

Likewise, Paul does not mean to imply that Jesus was in any way inferior to the Father but simply that He was willingly obedient to Him.

BLATANT FALSEHOOD

Another method of sabotaging the Scriptures which clearly express the deity of the Lord Jesus can be found in the Watchtower's treatment of John 8:58.

As we learned in the preceding chapter, this reference clearly illustrates the fact that Jesus is Jehovah when considered in the light of Moses' dialogue with Jehovah in the third chapter of Exodus.

The second verse of this chapter declares that it was the ANGEL OF THE LORD Who appeared unto Moses in the midst of the burning bush. We have ascertained that said angel is none other than the pre-incarnate Christ.

Further evidence for this is provided in verse fourteen where Jehovah calls Himself the I AM. In the passage in question (John 8:58), Jesus applies this same title to Himself which, of course, He was certainly entitled to do since, as we have seen, Exodus 3:2 demonstrates that it was indeed Christ Who was speaking with Moses.

When Jesus called Himself the I AM as recorded in John's Gospel, those who heard Him knew and understood that He was claiming to be the very One Who appeared to Moses on Mount Sinai and prepared to stone Him to death for this claim!

Naturally, the Watchtower had to do something about this passage!

But what could they possibly do? The passage is clear-cut and straightforward. What could they do indeed...

The Watchtower's response appeared to make sense and actually sounded quite scholarly.

A footnote appeared at the bottom of page 312 of the New World Translation of the Christian Greek Scriptures (Second Edition 1951) which stated that the passage in question should actually read, "I HAVE BEEN" rather than "I AM". This intelligent sounding assertion was based on, according to their footnote, "the perfect indefinite tense" of the original Greek.

So how do we know that the Watchtower is not correct in this assertion? How can we simply brush aside their argument without a proper and thorough study of it?

Quite easily. For you see, dear reader, there is no such thing as a "perfect indefinite tense" in the Greek language!

The Watchtower invented a Greek tense which does not even exist in order to change the clear message of John 8:58!

It is interesting to note that the Watchtower stopped printing the aforementioned footnote when this passage was pointed out to them. They continue to render the passage, "I have been", however.

This glaring deception is even more abrasive when one realizes that errors (or lies!) should never appear in footnotes since the entire purpose of the footnote is to verify and support the text!

A FEW GOOD QUESTIONS

Let us now respond to several queries which invariably work their way into any discussion on this topic. Although the first three questions differ, the same response can be used to answer all of them. Therefore, we shall list the first three questions together followed by the response:

If Jesus is God, to Whom did He pray?

If Jesus is God, to Whom did He call while on the cross?

If Jesus is God, Who ran the universe while He lay in the tomb?

Exigent questions all. Questions which form mental roadblocks in the minds of many Christians as well as cultists. Questions which cannot go unanswered.

Although the very nature of the queries would seem to necessitate very long, complex and drawn out explanations, the following basic response will prove adequate.

Simply put, the answer to the problems posed by the aforementioned inquiries lies in the existence of the blessed Trinity.

Herein lies the importance of a proper comprehension of the Godhead. Though Jesus, as we have seen, was fully man and fully God, He is still, nonetheless, only one-third of the Trinity. In other words, while Jesus suffered the crucifixion and succumbed to death, the Father and the Holy Spirit remained very much in control of the universe and all else.

Similarly, when Jesus prayed, as He so often did,

He was not "praying to Himself" as the cults sarcastically suggest, but was in fact praying directly to God the Father. By the same token, when He called out while dying on the cross He was calling to the Father (Luke 23:46).

There is absolutely no problem or contradiction within this discussion when the true Christian theology of the Godhead is considered.

Incidentally, the preceding questions and the response to them, while not overly-detailed, should effectively show the blatant error of the "Jesus Only" doctrine which is promulgated by the United Pentecostal organization.

WHY DIDN'T JESUS KNOW THE HOUR OF HIS RETURN?

Doesn't Jehovah know everything (Hebrews 4:13)?

According to Scripture, He does. Therefore, how can Jesus be Jehovah since He (Jesus) admitted to not knowing when He would return (Mark 13:31, 32) and in fact didn't even know who had touched His clothing as He walked (Mark 5:30)?

Philippians 2:5-8 offers our elucidation.

Christ, when He left His heavenly home in order

to be born of the virgin (John 1:14), voluntarily humbled Himself by limiting His attributes of deity. It must be understood that He was still very much God but in a self-restricted fashion.

Dr. Herbert Lockyer offers the following explanation:

> As the Eternal Word, He could not empty Himself either of His deity or His attributes. What He divested Himself of was the constant, outward and visible manifestation of His Godhead. Christ did not surrender deity – He gained humanity. Paul deals, not so much with what the Son gave up, but what He gained, namely, exaltation for humiliation. Assuming the name and role of a servant, He came to possess a name above every name. Dr. Ward quotes the Greek scholar, Dr. William Hersey Davis who suggested that 'the word kenoo should be understood in the sense of emptying one vessel into another vessel so that it was a matter of pouring the same content into another form: Christ emptied Himself, that is, poured Himself into the form of a servant. [31]

So we see that Jesus willingly set aside certain aspects of His deity when He took upon Himself "the

---

31 Taken from ALL THE DOCTRINES OF THE BIBLE by Herbert Lockyer. Copyright 1964 by the Zondervan Publishing House. Used by permission. p. 44.

form of a servant, and was made in the likeness of men...". Although this is a rather basic view of the subject, it should serve to assist the student in his/her understanding of it.

There is no doubt that we have barely scratched the surface of this vast area of cult apologetics. Many more passages could be considered and scrutinized, passages which the cults have twisted and damaged without regard for language, syntax, etymology, historicity or context.

Much more could be said from the standpoint of the original Hebrew and Greek texts which seem to hold no meaning whatsoever for many of the cults and sects of our day.

However, unlike some, I prefer to acknowledge my scholastic and linquistic limits and leave such topics to true Hebrew and Greek scholars.

In 1 Corinthians the Apostle Paul warned that there is "another Gospel....ANOTHER JESUS....". Even a cursory glance through the religious press of our day verifies the truth of this statement. There are, depending on which group one chooses to follow, many Jesuses. And it is imperative to know, beyond the shadow of a doubt, that we are following and trusting in the right one, the Jesus of the Scriptures.

I, for one, have always been quite amazed when reading the above Scripture passage….It could not be clearer. It is as though Paul is seeing the Watchtower, the Way International, the Mormons and others. It is as though he is calling out to all who will hear, "Yes, there is another Jesus….Be careful what you believe!"

Interestingly, many Witnesses are quite intrigued when this passage is carefully and lovingly pointed out to them. It comes as quite a surprise that the Bible itself warns of this "other Jesus". This fact can be quite helpful when attempting to lead them to the freedom and salvation that the Jesus of the Bible offers.

Hopefully the preceding examples have demonstrated the plentiful "straw men" within the world of the cults – Straw men which, although it may appear otherwise at times, do not really have all the answers…

Appendix One

The Personality And Deity Of The Holy Spirit

Having concluded that Scripture unequivocally teaches that Jesus Christ is Jehovah God, our next task is to ascertain whether or not the Bible attributes divinity to the Holy Spirit as well.

Endeavoring to know the Spirit, even as He is known, we must seek after a right adjustment to this Holy One Himself. A spiritual understanding is dependent upon instant and unfailing surrender to truth revealed.

While, of course, the Scriptures do not stop to prove the Spirit's reality, but plainly state the fact, yet because some are guilty, either from ignorance or thoughtlessness, of applying neuter pronouns to Him, or of speaking of Him simply as an influence, or an emanation, both of which are errors, so unscriptural and paralyzing to the most pungent exhortations based on the believer's new life in Christ, we deem it necessary (sic) to correct same. [1]

We have seen how the cults attempt to hide or take away from the deity of Jesus Christ and it should come as no surprise that similar tactics are used to deny the position of the Holy Spirit.

The majority of the cults teach that the Holy Spirit is not an individual nor a personality, but a "force", nothing more than an "energy mass". The Bible neither teaches nor supports this twisted fallacy.

THE HOLY SPIRIT – A PERSON OR "FORCE"?

Perhaps the major difficulty of those who choose to deny the personality of the Holy Spirit is their misunderstanding of the concept, due to the lack of a material body.

Dr. Lockyer responds...

---

1 Taken from ALL THE DOCTRINES OF THE BIBLE by Herbert Lockyer. Copyright 1964 by the Zondervan Publishing House. Used by permission. p. 72.

As we usually associate personality with a body, it is somewhat difficult to comprehend the Spirit's personality seeing He does not have a material form made up of hands, feet, eyes and mouth. What we are apt to forget is that these parts of the human frame are not characteristics of personality, although they are channels of such; they simply represent corporeity, that is, they belong entirely to the body.

True personality, then, is not the outward building but the tenant within. Personality is made up of distinctive features or elements known as heart, mind and will. 'Personality,' it has been said, 'is capacity for fellowship. The very quality which was most singularly characteristic of Jesus manifests itself in the Spirit, only more universally, more intimately, more surely.' Being able to think, feel and will, the Spirit has the capacity for fellowship, WHICH IS NOT POSSIBLE WITHOUT PERSONALITY. [2] (emphasis mine)

Let us begin this section of our study by considering the teachings of three of the more popular cults concerning the personality of the Holy Spirit.

Herbert W. Armstrong's Worldwide Church of God

[2] Taken from ALL THE DOCTRINES OF THE BIBLE by Herbert Lockyer. Copyright 1964 by the Zondervan Publishing House. Used by permission. Pgs. 75-76.

completely rejects the idea of the Holy Spirit being a personality and/or one of the blessed Trinity:

> But the theologians and 'Higher Critics' have blindly accepted THE HERETICAL AND FALSE DOCTRINE introduced by PAGAN FALSE PROPHETS who crept in, that the Holy Spirit is a third person... [3] (emphasis mine)

Also,

> Here, then, we have the simple truth of how God can be one God yet TWO (not three) persons... [4] (Brackets and emphasis mine)

The Way International has another outlook on the subject.

> Victor Paul Wierwille taught that when he capitalized the words "Holy Spirit", he was referring to God the Father since He (the Father) is both holy and spirit. However, according to Wierwille, when the words are not capitalized, it refers to the gifts of the spirit. [5]

The Jehovah's Witnesses teach that the Holy Spirit

---

3 Just What Do You Mean – Born Again? Herbert W. Armstrong: Pasadena, CA. Ambassador Press, n.d., pgs. 17, 19.

4 The Good News of the World Tomorrow, Vol. XXXIII, No. 7 article entitled: Just What is the Holy Spirit? Bernard W. Schnippert, p. 27.

5 From Victor Paul Wierwille and The Way International, by J.L. Williams. Copyright 1979. Moody Bible Institute of Chicago. Used by permission. p. 82.

is not a personality at all, but a "force" or "power".
Let them speak for themselves:

> As for the 'Holy Spirit', the so-called 'third Person of the Tinity', we have already seen that it is NOT A PERSON, but God's ACTIVE FORCE. [6] (emphasis mine)

Also,

> The Scriptures themselves unite to show that God's holy spirit IS NOT A PERSON but is God's ACTIVE FORCE by which he accomplishes his purpose and executes his will. [7] (emphasis mine)

Does the Bible support any of the above theories? We shall examine several Scripture references in an attempt to find the answer.

According to Lockyer...

> There are some 160 passages in the Old and New Testaments bearing upon the actions of the Holy Spirit, and to deny personality to Him is to make these references meaningless and absurd... [8]

---

6 The Truth That Leads to Eternal Life, Brooklyn: Watchtower Bible and Tract Society, 1968, p. 24.

7 Aid to Bible Understanding, Brooklyn: Watchtower Bible and Tract Society, 1969, 1971, p. 1543.

8 Taken from ALL THE DOCTRINES OF THE BIBLE by Herbert Lockyer. Copyright 1964 by the Zondervan Publishing House. Used by permission. p. 77.

SCRIPTURE ASCRIBES PERSONALITY TO THE HOLY SPIRIT

First of all, the reader is invited to consider the following passages which clearly show that the Holy Spirit does indeed possess attributes of personality.

Beginning with John's Gospel we find many instances of the Holy Spirit being referred to as a personality (i.e., he, him):

> Even the Spirit of truth; whom the world cannot receive, because it seeth HIM not, neither knoweth HIM: but ye know HIM; for HE dwelleth with you, and shall be in you. (14:17)

> But the Comforter, which is the Holy Ghost, WHOM the Father will send in my name, HE shall teach you all things, and bring all things to your remembrance, whatsoever I have said unto you. (14:26)

> But when the Comforter is come, WHOM I will send unto you from the Father, even the Spirit of truth, which proceedeth from the Father, HE shall testify of me. (15:26)

> Nevertheless I tell you the truth; it is expedient for you that I go away: for if I go not away, the Comforter will not come unto you; but if

I depart, I will send HIM unto you. And when HE is come, HE will reprove the world of sin, and of righteousness, and of judgment. (16:7, 8)

The Book of Acts offers the following:

As they ministered to the Lord, and fasted, the Holy Ghost said, Separate ME Barnabas and Saul for the work whereunto I have called them. (13:2) (emphasis in all above Scripture is mine)

In the passages listed, the Holy Spirit has been called "HE", "HIM", "WHOM" and "I". Consider the absurdity of referring to a "force" or "power" in this manner.

Dr. Walter Martin has correctly stated,

Attributes which can only be ascribed to a person are ascribed to the Holy Spirit.[9]

We shall now consider some of the aforementioned attributes.

For the Holy Ghost shall TEACH you in the same hour what ye ought to say. (Luke 12:12)

---

9 Martin Speaks Out on the Cults. Walter R. Martin. Ventura, Calif. Vision House Publishers, 1983, p. 42.

...He (the Holy Spirit) shall TEACH you all things, AND BRING ALL THINGS TO YOUR REMEBRANCE, whatsoever I have said unto you. (John 14:26)

He (the Holy Spirit) shall TESTIFY of me. (John 15:26)

And when He (the Holy Spirit) is come, he will REPROVE the world of sin, and of righteousness, and of judgment. (John 16:8)

While Peter thought on the vision, the Spirit SAID unto him, Behold, three men seek thee. Arise therefore, and get thee down, and go with them, doubting nothing: for I HAVE SENT THEM. (Acts 10:19, 20)

...The Holy Ghost SAID, Separate me Barnabas and Saul for the work whereunto I HAVE CALLED THEM. (Acts 13:2)

For it SEEMED GOOD TO THE HOLY GHOST, and to us, to lay upon you no greater burden than these necessary things. (Acts 15:28)

And when he was come unto us, he took Paul's girdle, and bound his own hands and feet, and said, Thus SAITH THE HOLY GHOST....(Acts 21:11)

Likewise the Spirit also HELPETH our infirmities: for we know not what we should pray for as we ought: but the Spirit itself MAKETH INTERCESSION for us with GROANINGS which cannot be uttered. (Romans 8:26)

But God hath revealed them unto us by his Spirit: for the Spirit SEARCHETH all things, yea, the deep things of God. (1 Corinthians 2:10)

But all these worketh that one and the self-same Spirit, dividing to every man severally AS HE WILL. (1 Corinthians 12:11)

And GRIEVE not the Holy Spirit of God, whereby ye are sealed unto the day of redemption. (Ephesians 4:30) (brackets and emphasis in all above Scripture are mine)

From the previously listed passages we learn that the Holy Spirit "TEACHES", "BRINGS THINGS TO REMEMBRANCE (reminds)", "TESTIFIES", "REPROVES", "SPEAKS", "SENDS", "CALLS", "SENSES", "HELPS", "MAKES INTERCESSION", "GROANS", "SEARCHES", "DIVIDES", "WILLS", and, He can be "GRIEVED". Again, could a "force" or "power" do these things?

Lockyer points out the following:

Language has no meaning if the Spirit is not a Person, seeing that Jesus repeatedly employed the masculine pronoun when speaking of Him. Thirteen times over, in John 16, for example, He refers to the Spirit as He, Him, Himself. As the 'Advocate' He holds an office only possible to a Person.... [10]

THE DEITY OF THE HOLY SPIRIT

Having reached this point, it is felt that the reader has been provided with sufficient data to prove the personality of the Holy Spirit. We now direct ourselves to the question of His deity. Dr. John F. Walvoord has this to say:

In the sacred Scriptures, the evidence for the deity of the Holy Spirit is superabundant. In general the doctrine is supported by the names and titles of the Holy Spirit, His identification and association with God, His procession and relation to the holy Trinity, His divine attributes, and His many divine works. These combine to confirm and enhance the significant contribution of each to the whole and harmonize in a great symphony of Scriptural testimony. [11]

10 Taken from ALL THE DOCTRINES OF THE BIBLE by Herbert Lockyer. Copyright 1964 by the Zondervan Publishing House. Used by permission. p. 76.

11 Taken from THE HOLY SPIRIT by John F. Walvoord. Copyright 1954 by Van Kampen Press, Copyright 1958 by Dunham Publishing Company. Used by permission of Zonder-

THE HOLY SPIRIT'S ROLE IN CREATION

We have already established the fact that Jesus Christ is the Creator (see John 1:1-3; Colossians 1:16, 17 and Hebrews 1:1, 2), and we also know that Genesis 1:1 teaches that God made the heaven and earth. Consequently, Jesus the Creator IS God the Creator. But does the Bible include the Holy Spirit in the creation account?

Consider Genesis 1:2,

> "And the SPIRIT of God moved upon the face of the waters." (emphasis mine)

This Scripture shows that the Holy Spirit was in fact active in the creation. But let's not rely on a singular reference. Consider also Elihu's comment,

> "THE SPIRIT OF GOD HATH MADE ME..." (Job 33:4, emphasis mine)

The Holy Spirit's role in creation is also inculcated in the Psalms,

> "Thou sendest forth thy SPIRIT, they are created...." (104:30, emphasis mine)

> In the work of creation itself, then, the Holy Spirit is revealed to have a distinct character

of operation. He brings order to creation; He is the giver of life; and shapes creation to achieve its significant purpose of bringing glory to God. [12]

Again, referring to Walvoord, we read,

A second important line of proof for the creative work of the Holy Spirit is found in the use of the word Elohim for the Creator. The term is properly plural as demonstrated by its use in reference to the plurality of heathen gods. Some have tried to explain away this evidence for the Trinity in the Old Testament, speaking of this use of the plural as the plural of majesty, citing the English idiom of waters (plural) for water (singular) in poetic expression to give the impression of greatness or extent. In view of the abundant testimony to the trinity not only in the New Testament but in the Old Testament as well, it is fitting that a name for God should be used which should express the plural idea of the persons of the Godhead. NOT A SINGLE GOOD REASON HAS EVER BEEN ADVANCED FOR NOT REGARDING THIS PLURAL AS GENUINE. The arguments against it have been Unitarian, Jewish, or from liberal theology. The plural term

12 Taken from THE HOLY SPIRIT by John F. Walvoord. Copyright 1954 by Van Kampen Press, Copyright 1958 by Dunham Publishing Company. Used by permission of Zondervan Publishing House. p. 42.

for God thus found so prominently in the creation narrative constitutes an important contribution to the creative work of the Holy Spirit.

Every use of the term implies a work not only of any one person, but of all three persons. Hence in Genesis 1:1, where it speaks of God creating, it is speaking of the Trinity explicitly, not only conceived of as one essence, but as the Triune God. Every work attributed to God under this term is accordingly an assertion of a ministry of the Holy Spirit. If we had no other reference to the creative work of the Holy Spirit than this use of the plural term, it would justify the doctrine, even though it would not reveal anything distinctive concerning the Spirit. [13]

THE ETERNALITY OF THE SPIRIT

If the Holy Spirit is indeed God, He would, of necessity be everlasting. Does the Bible support this thought?

How much more shall the blood of Christ, who through the ETERNAL SPIRIT offered

---

13 Taken from THE HOLY SPIRIT by John F. Walvoord. Copyright 1954 by Van Kampen Press, Copyright 1958 by Dunham Publishing Company. Used by permission of Zondervan Publishing House. p. 39.

himself without spot to God, purge your conscience from dead works to serve the living God? (Hebrews 9:14, emphasis mine)

THE SPIRIT'S ROLE IN THE RESURRECTION OF CHRIST

We have also learned that both the Father and Christ raised Jesus from the dead (Acts 3:26; 1 Thessalonians 1:10 and John 2:19-21). But Romans 8:11 and 1 Peter 3:18 both teach that the Holy Spirit raised Jesus to life! Consequently the Bible clearly teaches that all three Persons of the Trinity were instrumental in the Lord's resurrection!

BLASPHEMY AGAINST..."A FORCE"?

Allow me to point out an interesting aspect of the Holy Ghost. Matthew 12 indicates an extremely important position of the Holy Spirit which I dare say would never be attributed to a mere "force" or "power":

Wherefore I say unto you, ALL MANNER of sin and blasphemy shall be forgiven unto men; BUT THE BLASPHEMY AGAINST THE HOLY GHOST SHALL NOT BE FORGIVEN UNTO MEN. And whosoever speaketh a word against the Son of man, it shall be forgiven him; BUT WHOSOEVER SPEAKETH AGAINST THE HOLY GHOST, IT

SHALL NOT BE FORGIVEN HIM, NEITHER
IN THIS WORLD, NEITHER IN THE WORLD
TO COME. (vs. 31, 32, emphasis mine)

Similarly, Romans 8:9 shares an important thought
on the Holy Spirit:

> But ye are not in the flesh, but in the Spirit,
> if so be that the Spirit of God dwell in you.
> Now if any man HAVE NOT THE SPIRIT of
> Christ, he is none of his. (emphasis mine)

The author finds it difficult to believe that such a
tremendous value could be placed on an imper-
sonal "mass of energy".

COMPARING SCRIPTURE WITH SCRIPTURE

Perhaps the most convincing portion of Scripture
would be 2 Peter 1:20, 21, which says:

> Knowing this first, that no prophecy of the
> scripture is of any private interpretation. For
> the prophecy came not in old time by the will
> of man: but holy men of God spake as they
> were moved BY THE HOLY GHOST. (em-
> phasis mine)

The significance of this passage becomes apparent
when it is cross-referenced with 2 Timothy 3:16;

"ALL SCRIPTURE is given by inspiration OF GOD..." (emphasis mine)

Once again we are confronted with the question, does the Bible contradict itself?

Apparently it does. One Scripture teaches that the Holy Spirit inspired the Bible while another passage teaches that God inspired ALL Scripture...Unless the Holy Spirit is God!

LYING TO...."A POWER"?

The fifth chapter of the Book of Acts offers some interesting food for thought. It would be profitable to consider several verses at this point in our study.

> But a certain man named Ananias, with Sapphira his wife, sold a possession, And kept back part of the price, his wife also being privy to it, and brought a certain part, and laid it at the apostles' feet. But Peter said, Ananias, why hath Satan filled thine heart TO LIE TO THE HOLY GHOST, and to keep back part of the price of the land? Whiles it remained, was it not thine own? And after it was sold, was it not in thine own power? Why hast thou conceived this thing in thine heart? Thou hast not lied unto men, BUT UNTO GOD. (vs. 1-4, emphasis mine)

The above portion of Scripture teaches two important details. First of all, the reader will notice that Peter first accused Ananias of lying to the Holy Ghost (v. 3), but later pointed out that he (Ananias) had actually lied to God (v. 4). The straight-forwardness of this passage cannot be denied. By lying to the Holy Ghost, Ananias had lied to God. This could be possible, quite simply, only if the Holy Spirit is God!

Secondly, even if the cultist chooses to ignore the above implications, he/she must consider the fact that Peter plainly declared that the Holy Spirit had been lied to! I am obliged to point out the doltishness of the concept of lying to a "force" or "energy mass". To do so would be similar to lying to a car, a closet door, a frying pan or any other "thing". Indeed, it is true that only a cognizant personality can be lied to.*

COMPARING THE OLD TESTAMENT WITH THE NEW

Another intriguing analysis of the deity of the Holy Spirit can be had by comparing the Old Testament with the New. For example, Isaiah 6:8, 9 reads:

> Also I heard the voice OF THE LORD, saying, Whom shall I send, and who will go for

* Note: The account of Ananias and Sapphira is translated expediently in the New World Translation.

us? Then said I, Here am I; send me. And he (the Lord) said Go, and tell this people …. (brackets and emphasis mine)

So we see that the prophet Isaiah was, of course, commissioned by Jehovah. But when Paul quotes the writing of Isaiah mentioned above, he credits the call to the Holy Ghost:

…. Well spake THE HOLY GHOST by Esaias (Isaiah) the prophet unto our fathers, Saying, Go…. (Acts 28:25, 26, brackets and emphasis mine)

With the above in mind, we consider the words of Dr. George Smeaton:

We NOWHERE read that God first revealed something to the Holy Spirit as if He were not consubstantial with God Himself, and then charged Him to convey the communication to the prophet. On the contrary, while there is a certain order of subsistence and operation in the Godhead, the Spirit of God is always spoken of as possessing divine intelligence, omnipotence, and omnipresence; and all the prophecies are uniformly spoken of as THE IMMEDIATE ACT OF GOD HIMSELF. [14] (emphasis mine)

---

14 Taken from THE DOCTRINE OF THE HOLY SPIRIT by George Smeaton. Copyright 1980, Banner of Truth Edition. p. 265. Used by permission.

Again we are forced to ruminate the same decision. Either the Bible is incorrect and indeed quite fallible because it contradicts itself by saying that Jehovah said something, and then, in another location credits the Holy Spirit with the quotation. Or, there is no contradiction because the Holy Spirit is Jehovah and therefore the quote can be accredited to either one!

Knowing that the Bible is 100% correct and infallible, I choose to cling tenaciously to the latter.

We refer to Walvoord for a succinct summation:

> The Scriptural revelation concerning the attributes of the Holy Spirit points unmistakably to conclusion that the Holy Spirit possesses full deity. This can be demonstrated in at least seven particulars:

(1) The Holy Spirit is revealed as possessing life (Rom. 8:2). The context indicates spiritual or eternal life is in view, which, originally, was the possession of God alone, now bestowed on some of His creatures through regeneration.
(2) The attribute of personality has abundant witness as already demonstrated.
(3) The Holy Spirit is omnipresent (Ps. 139:7), an attribute only God may possess.
(4) Omniscience belongs to the Holy Spirit (1 Cor. 2:10-11), and

(5)omnipotence, as illustrated in His work of creation (Gen. 1:2).

(6)Holiness is frequently assigned the One who is distinctively known as the Holy Spirit (Luke 11:13).

(7)The eternity of the Spirit is revealed also in Scripture (Heb. 9:14). The nature of the attributes are such that they could not all be communicated to a creature. From the explicit revelation of the attributes of the Holy Spirit, it may be concluded that His deity is fully sustained in Scripture. [15]

Our inescapable conclusion then, based upon the Word of God, is that the Bible irrefutably teaches that the Holy Spirit is deity.

---

15 Taken from THE HOLY SPIRIT by John F. Walvoord. Copyright 1954 by Van Kampen Press, Copyright 1958 by Dunham Publishing Company. Used by permission of Zondervan Publishing House. Pgs. 16-17.

Appendix Two

THE TRINITY

Of all the doctrines in the Word of God, perhaps none is as difficult, indeed impossible, to fully comprehend as is the doctrine of the Trinity.

The cultist is quick to attack it simply because it cannot be explained to the satisfaction of all, or due to the fact that the Bible appears to contradict itself by stating that the Lord is one, while also asserting the tri-unity of the Godhead.

Dr. Emery H. Bancroft aptly responds:

1. The mode of this triune existence is inscru-

table. It is inscrutable because there are no analogies to it in our finite experience. For this reason, all attempts to represent it adequately are vain.

(a) From inanimate things – as the fountain, the stream, and the rivulet, trickling from it; the cloud, the rain, and the rising mist; color, shape, and size; the actinic, luminiferous, and calorific principles in a ray of the sun.

(b) From the constitution or processes of our minds – as the psychological unity of intellect, affection, and will; the logical unity of thesis, antithesis, and synthesis; the metaphysical unity of subject, object, and subject-object.

(c) No one of these furnishes any proper analogue of the Trinity, since in no one of them is found the essential element of tripersonality. Such illustrations may sometime be used to disarm objection, but they furnish no positive explanation of the mystery of the Trinity and unless carefully guarded may lead to grievous error.

2. The doctrine of the Trinity is not self-contradictory. This it would be only if it declared God to be Three in the same numerical sense in

which He is said to be One. This we do not assert. We assert simply that the same God who is one with respect to His essence is three with respect to internal distinctions of that essence, or with respect to the modes of His being. The possibility of this cannot be denied, except by assuming that the human mind is in all respects the measure of the divine. The fact that the ascending scale of life is marked by increasing differentiation of faculty and function would rather lead us to expect, in the highest of all beings, a nature more complex than our own. [1]

J.L. Williams offers the following:

Tritheism is not trinitarianism. Please remember that important distinction. Tritheism is a belief in three distinct gods, whereas trinitarianism is a belief in three Persons, but one God. [2]

The preceding statement is of very great importance, for as we will see, the main reason for the denial of the Trinity on the part of the cultist is due to his or her lack of understanding of the true theology of the Christian Church on the subject.

---

1 Taken from CHRISTIAN THEOLOGY (Second Edition) by Emery H. Bancroft. Published by Zondervan Publishing House. Copyright 1976, Baptist Bible College & Seminary. Used by permission. Pgs. 88-89.

2 From Victor Paul Wierwille and The Way International by J.L. Williams. Copyright 1979, Moody Bible Institute of Chicago. Used by permission. p. 78.

WHAT THE CULTS BELIEVE

Charles Taze Russell, founder of the Jehovah's Witnesses expressed this blatant lack of understanding when he wrote,

> ...Sincere persons who want to know the true God and serve Him find it a bit difficult to love and worship a complicated...freakishlooking, three-headed God. [3]

It is paramount that the reader understand the true Christian belief regarding the Trinity if he or she is to efficaciously assist the cultist who has been deceived and confused as to what the Christian Church actually believes and teaches. However, before responding to the above quotation of the Watchtower, let us consider the opinions of others as well.

The Way International makes no attempt to conceal their opposition to the teaching of the Holy Trinity or Godhead;

> Trinitarian dogma degrades God from his elevated unparalleled position, besides it leaves man unredeemed. [4]

---

3 Let God be True. Brooklyn, New York. Watchtower Bible and Tract Society, 1946 ed. p. 102.

4 Taken from frontspiece of Jesus Christ is Not God. Victor Paul Wierwille, 1981, New Knoxville, Ohio, American Christian Press.

The Unity School of Christianity has this to say about the Trinity,

> The Father is Principle, the Son is that Principle revealed in the creative plan, the Holy Spirit is the executive power of both Father and Son carrying out the plan. [5]

According to the Christian Scientist....

> The theory of three persons in one God (that is, a personal Trinity or Tri-unity) suggests polytheism, rather than the one ever-present I AM. [6] (brackets and emphasis mine)

Armstrong's Worldwide Church of God also argues against the Trinity doctrine by stating;

> I suppose most people think of God as one single individual Person. Or, as a 'trinity'. THIS IS NOT TRUE.... [7] (emphasis mine)

Referring once again to the Watchtower, we see just how far they go in their attempts to dismiss the Biblical teaching of the Godhead;

> The doctrine, in brief, is that there are __THREE GODS__ IN ONE: 'God the Father,

5 Metaphysical Bible Dictionary, Unity School of Christianity, p. 629.

6 Science and Health, With Key to the Scriptures. Mary Baker Eddy, p. 256.

7 Just What do you Mean — Born Again? Herbert W. Armstrong. Pasadena, CA. Ambassador Press. p. 17.

God the Son, and God the Holy Ghost', all three equal in power, substance and eternity. [8](emphasis mine)

Also from the Watchtower,

The obvious conclusion is, therefore, that SATAN IS THE ORIGINATOR OF THE TRINITY DOCTRINE. [9](emphasis mine)

As previously mentioned and evidenced by the preceding quotes, the difficulty here lies in the cultist's misinterpretation of the Scriptural teachings of the Christian Church regarding the Trinity. Once again, the orthodox Christian teaching IS NOT a belief in three gods, but rather three Persons Who comprise the one God.

It would be good to consider an excellent explanation of the Church's actual doctrine of the Trinity as set forth by Josh McDowell:

One of the most misunderstood ideas in the Bible concerns the teaching about the Trinity. Although Christians say that they believe in one God, they are constantly accused of polytheism (worshipping at least three gods).

The Scriptures do not teach that there are

8 Let God be True. Brooklyn; Watchtower Bible and Tract Society, 1946 ed. p. 100.

9 Let God be True. Brooklyn; Watchtower Bible and Tract Society, 1946 ed. p. 101.

three Gods; neither do they teach that God wears three different masks while acting out the drama of history. What the Bible does teach is stated in the doctrine of the Trinity as: there is one God who has revealed Himself in three persons, the Father, the Son and the Holy Spirit, and these three persons are the one God.

Although this is difficult to comprehend, it is nevertheless what the Bible tells us, and is the closest the finite mind can come to explaining the infinite mystery of the infinite God, when considering the biblical statements about God's being. [10]

THE TRINITY IN CREATION

As we have noticed, the first verse of the Bible proclaims that, "In the beginning God created the heaven and the earth" (Genesis 1:1). It is worthwhile to point out at this time that the Hebrew word for God used in this text is Elohim which is plural, not singular, and is repeated no less than thirty-two times in chapter one.

The New World Translation asserts that this implies "the excellence of majesty" but we have absolutely

10 Josh McDowell and Don Stewart, HANDBOOK OF TODAY'S RELIGIONS: Understanding the Cults, p. 33. Copyright 1982, Campus Crusade for Christ. Published by Here's Life Publishers. Used with permission.

no proof to support such an assertion. We must ask ourselves why Moses, under the direction of the Holy Spirit, would choose to use the plural form of the word when it would have been a simple matter to use the singular. [11]

Further support is given to this logic when the words of the Lord as recorded in Genesis 1:26 are considered, "Let US make man in OUR image, after OUR likeness..." (emphasis mine)

Quite expectedly, the Jehovah's Witnesses are quick to quote Deuteronomy 6:4 in a frail attempt to disprove the Trinity, "Hear, O Israel: The Lord our God is one Lord", but it must be noted that the word used in this text for one is "echad" which means "united one", NOT "yachid" which means absolute mathematical oneness." [12]

Dr. Smeaton approaches the subject thusly;

> 'Let US make man in our image, after our likeness' (Gen. 1:26). The use of the plural number in the pronoun US is not to be reduced, according to the evacuating principle of Rationalism, to a mere mannerism in style. Dr. Owen has well remarked that God, having manifested by other parts of creation His existence, nature, and perfections, designed

---

11 See also What Every Jehovah's Witness Should Know by Arthur M. Bowser. Accent Publications, Denver, Colorado, 1978, p. 16.

12 Ibid. p. 17.

in the creation of man to manifest Himself in a trinity of persons; a remark setting forth a momentous truth only too little pondered. [13]

THE TRINITY DOCTRINE IS SCRIPTURAL

The reader may be aware that there exist several other passages of Scripture which present the same tri-unity of God;

> And the Lord God said, Behold, the man is become AS ONE OF US, to know good and evil...(Genesis 3:22, emphasis mine)

> Go to, let US go down, and there confound their language... (Genesis 11:7, emphasis mine)

> ...Whom shall I (Jehovah) send, and who will go FOR US? (Isaiah 6:8, brackets and emphasis mine)

We could not consider a study of the Trinity complete without also examining the great commission of Matthew 28.

> Go ye therefore, and teach all nations, baptizing them in the name of the Father, and of

---

13 Taken from THE DOCTRINE OF THE HOLY SPIRIT, by George Smeaton. Copyright 1980, Banner of Truth Edition, p. 11. Used by permission.

the Son, and of the Holy Ghost. (v. 19)

It is apparent that Jesus fully believed and accepted the reality of all three Persons of the Godhead and it becomes increasingly convincing when one considers the fact that Jesus said to baptize "in the name" (singular), even though three individuals are mentioned!

F.W. Thomas provides a provocative thought:

> Let us read this text using the JW (Jehovah's Witnesses) definition of the Son and the Holy Spirit. (Keep in mind that the JW's define Christ as a mere creature and the Holy Spirit as just an active force.) Our text would then read:

> 'Baptizing them in the name of the Father, and of a Creature, and of an Active Force.' Such a rendering creates a grating effect and is most blasphemous. Paul in his benediction also refers to the Trinity: 'The grace of the Lord Jesus Christ, and the love of God, and the communion of the Holy Ghost, be with you all' (2 Cor. 13:14). The same intolerable discord presents itself if we attempt to interpret this text according to JW teaching: 'The grace of a Creature, and the love of God, and the communion of an Active Force, be with you all.' How terribly

distorted these scriptures become when we interpret them according to JW theology! [14] (first brackets mine)

Note too, that all three Persons of the Trinity were present at both the birth and baptism of Jesus.

The Holy Ghost (Third Person of the Trinity) shall come upon thee, and the power of the Highest shall overshadow thee: therefore also that holy thing that shall be born of thee shall be called the Son (Second Person of the Trinity) of God (The Father – First Person of the Trinity). (Luke 1:35, brackets mine)

And it came to pass in those days, that Jesus came from Nazareth of Galilee, and was baptized of John in the Jordan. And straightway coming up out of the water, he saw the heavens opened, and the Spirit (Third Person of the Trinity) like a dove, descending upon him: And there came a voice from heaven, saying, Thou are my beloved Son (Jesus – Second Person of the Trinity), in whom I (Father – First Person of the Trinity) am well pleased. (Mark 1:9-11, brackets mine)

---

14 Taken from MASTERS OF DECEPTION by F. W. Thomas. Published by Baker Book House, Grand Rapids, Michigan, 1985, p. 8. Used by permission.

WHAT ABOUT THE MORMONS?

It is interesting to note that the Church of Jesus Christ of Latter Day Saints (Mormons), although claiming to accept the Bible as the Word of God, totally disregard all the implications of the aforementioned Scriptures. This fact becomes even harder to accept when one learns that the Mormons also deny the Trinity, while their own Book of Mormon fully supports the doctrine!

> And after this manner shall ye baptize in my name; for behold, verily I say unto you, that the Father, and the Son, and the Holy Ghost ARE ONE; and I am in the Father, and the Father in me, and the Father and I ARE ONE. (Book of Mormon – III Nephi 11:27, emphasis mine)

Also from the Book of Mormon:

> And thus will the Father bear record of me, and the Holy Ghost will bear record unto him of the Father and me; for the Father, and I, and the Holy Ghost ARE ONE. (III Nephi 11:36, emphasis mine)

It is difficult to imagine how the cults can so blatantly ignore whichever passages of Scripture they choose, but it is still more difficult to understand how they can similarly by-pass references in their own publications which support the Biblical teachings which they so adamantly argue against!

IT CANNOT BE IGNORED

It is of the utmost importance that the cultist be brought to the place where he or she understands the fact that we (Christians) do not believe in a strange, three-headed creature as the Jehovah's Witnesses erroneously report. Nor do we believe in a multiplicity of gods, as do the Mormons. Rather, we believe in one True and Almighty God Who exists in three distinct Persons – the Father, the Son, and the Holy Spirit.

I believe a very effective way to consider the topic of the Trinity is to grasp the fact that the Trinity is NOT tri-plex:

$$1+1+1=3$$

But tri-une:

$$1 \times 1 \times 1 = 1$$

Again referring to Evans;

> The doctrine of the Trinity is, in its last analysis, a deep mystery that cannot be fathomed

by the finite mind. That it is taught in the Scripture, however, there can be no reasonable doubt. It is a doctrine to be believed even though it cannot be thoroughly understood. [15]

---

15 Taken from THE GREAT DOCTRINES OF THE BIBLE by William Evans (enlarged edition). Used by permission, Moody Bible Institute of Chicago. Chicago, Ill., 1974, p. 27.

Appendix Three

THE RESURRECTION OF JESUS CHRIST

Another major doctrine of the Christian Church which is commonly scorned by several of the cults today is the resurrection of the Lord Jesus from the dead.

Did Christ rise from the tomb? If so, did He rise bodily or simply as a spirit? Does it really matter?

As is proper, we shall attempt to find the answers to the above listed questions in the Bible. Although God's Word is abundantly clear on the topic, the resurrection of Jesus is a predominant point of argument with the cults.

Dr. William Evans points out that....

> Christianity is the only religion that bases its claim to acceptance upon the resurrection of its founder. For any other religion to base its claim on such a doctrine would be to court failure. [1]

WHAT DO THE CULTS SAY?

In order to fully understand what we are dealing with in this instance, perhaps a brief look at the teachings of three or four of the more popular cults should be considered.

The Jehovah's Witnesses teach that....

> The firstborn (Christ) from the dead was raised from the grave, NOT A HUMAN CREATURE, BUT A SPIRIT. [2] (Brackets and emphasis mine)

Also,

> So the King Christ Jesus was put to death in the flesh and was resurrected AN INVISIBLE SPIRIT CREATURE. [3] (emphasis mine)

1 Taken from THE GREAT DOCTRINES OF THE BIBLE by William Evans (enlarged edition). Used by permission, Moody Bible Institute of Chicago. Chicago, Ill., 1974, p.84.

2 Let God be True. Brooklyn: Watchtower Bible and Tract Society, 1952 ed., p. 276

3 Let God be True. Brooklyn: Watchtower Bible and Tract Society, 1952 ed., p. 138.

The Unity School of Christianity mentions in its Statement of Faith,

> We believe the dissolution of spirit, soul and body, caused by death, is annulled by re-birth of the same spirit and soul in another body here on earth. We believe the repeated reincarnations of man are the merciful pro-vision of our loving Father to the end that all may come to obtain immortality through regeneration, AS DID JESUS. [4] (emphasis mine)

The Unification Church believes and teaches that Jesus' resurrection was not bodily. Instead, like the Watchtower, they believe that He was raised from the dead as a spirit. [5]

SPIRITUAL OR BODILY?

To begin, we must take into consideration the fact that each and every verse in the Bible which deals with the resurrection of the dead, including Jesus, refers exclusively to the body and never to a spirit or spiritual resurrection. In fact, in both the original Hebrew and Greek, the word resurrection is never applied to the soul or spirit of man.

4 Unity Statement of Faith (Lee's Summit, Mo.: Unity School of Christianity, n.d.), part 22.

5 THE DIVINE PRINCIPLE. Sun Myung Moon. Washington, D.C. Holy Spirit Association for the Unification of World Christianity, 1973, p. 36.

With this in mind, the reader is encouraged to consider the following fictitious illustration:

A young girl has just died. She is lying in the street, and a crowd gathers around her. News of what has happened reaches her parents and they rush to get to their daughter.

By the time they reach her, the group of onlookers has grown noticeably. A police officer, as well as an ambulance arrive shortly after the parents. The pale, limp, lifeless body is carefully examined and then strapped onto the ambulance stretcher. However, just as the paramedics prepare to lift the stretcher into the vehicle, a man steps forward from the crowd and introduces himself as a Christian miracle worker who can raise the girl from the dead!

At first, the girl's father is furious. How dare this stranger attempt to joke about such misfortune! But within seconds the grief-stricken mother convinces her husband to let the man try. After all, they have nothing to lose and she wants her child back, at any cost.

The crowd grows silent. The man steps toward the uncaring corpse and begins to pray. Not long thereafter he rises from his knees with a huge smile and shouts, "Praise the Lord! The little one has risen! She is no longer dead, she's alive!"

The crowd is shocked. The parents are crushed. What is this man saying? The girl is very obviously dead! The "miracle worker" is confronted by the angry father, but he holds to his story. "She is alive! She is risen! Although her body is still cold and lifeless, your daughter has been resurrected as an invisible spirit creature!"

Imagine the sorrow and disbelief of the parents. They wanted their daughter to live again as she had lived before. They wanted to be able to converse with her, to play with her, to enjoy her company. But they couldn't....She was still dead.

Ridiculous, isn't it? Yet this is exactly what the Jehovah's Witnesses expect us to believe about Jesus. According to the Watchtower, Jesus was raised from the dead, but not at all as He had been. He is now nothing more than a "spirit creature". He is not the same as the Jesus Who was crucified.

JESUS SAID HE WOULD RAISE...HIS BODY

Let us begin our study of what the Bible has to say on the subject by considering what Christ Himself said regarding His resurrection.

> Jesus answered and said unto them, Destroy this temple, and in three days I will raise it up. Then said the Jews, Forty and six years

was this temple in building, and wilt though rear it up in three days? But he spake of the temple OF HIS BODY. (John 2:19-21, emphasis mine)

It is interesting to note that the New World Translation clearly expresses the same fact of Christ's declaration of His BODILY resurrection in this passage.

As Dr. Martin points out,

> The Greek word soma is translated 'body' throughout the New Testament, so it is an inescapable fact that Christ was referring to his own physical form – hence a bodily resurrection. [6]

Several Scriptures seem to have been provided by the Lord for the specific purpose of clearly teaching the fact that Jesus' body overcame the power of death and was raised back to life.

For example, as previously considered, Thomas refused to believe that the Lord had risen from the grave until he had actually seen and TOUCHED Him. He was able to do this when Christ appeared before him IN THE SAME BODY that had been crucified and told Thomas to thrust his finger into

6 Gospel tract entitled Jehovah's Witnesses and the Resurrection of Jesus Christ. Walter R. Martin, American Tract Society, Garland, Texas. Reprinted by permission.

the holes that had been made by the nails and the spear (John 20:27).

Additional evidence to support the bodily resurrection of Jesus is found in Mark's Gospel where we read,

> "....He is risen, he is not here: behold the place where they laid him." (16:6), and Luke 24:3, "And they entered in (to the tomb) and FOUND NOT THE BODY OF THE LORD JESUS." (brackets and emphasis mine)

Again referring to Evans,

> The fact that the tomb was empty is testified to by competent witnesses – both friends and enemies: by the women, the disciples, the angels, and the Roman guards. How shall we account for the absence of the body of Jesus from the tomb? That it had not been stolen by outside parties is evident from the testimony of the soldiers who were bribed to tell that story (Matt. 28:11-15). Such a guard never would have allowed such a thing to take place. Their lives would have been thereby jeopardized. And if they were asleep (v. 13), how could they know what took place? Their testimony under such circumstances would be useless.

The condition in which the linen cloths were found lying by those who entered the tomb precludes the possibility of the body being stolen. Had such been the case the cloths would have been taken with the body, and not left in perfect order, thereby showing that the body had gone out of them. Burglars do not leave things in such perfect order. There is no order in haste.

Then again, we have the testimony of angels to the fact that Jesus had really risen as foretold (Matt. 28:6; Mark 16:6). The testimony of angels is surely trustworthy (Heb. 2:2). [7]

These Scriptures unite to form an imperative question – If Christ rose from the grave as a spirit, as the cultists claim, and His body did NOT rise from the grave, what happened to it?

The Watchtower offers the very feeble explanation that His body was either preserved as some kind of museum piece, or dissolved into gases. [8] However, neither of these hypotheses are acceptable in the light of the previously considered fact that Christ appeared after His death and burial IN THE SAME BODY that was crucified!

---

7 Taken from THE GREAT DOCTRINES OF THE BIBLE by William Evans (enlarged edition). Used by permission, Moody Bible Institute of Chicago. Chicago, Ill., 1974, p. 87.

8 Studies in the Scriptures, Vol. 2, p. 129. Watchtower Bible and Tract Society, Brooklyn, N.Y.

Perhaps the most vociferous Scripture to support the Christian view of the resurrection is Luke 24:36-43;

> And as they thus spake, Jesus himself stood in the midst of them, and saith unto them, Peace be unto you. But they were terrified and affrighted, and SUPPOSED THAT THEY HAD SEEN A SPIRIT. And he said unto them, Why are ye troubled? And why do thoughts arise in your hearts? Behold my hands and my feet, that it is I myself: HANDLE ME, AND SEE: FOR A SPIRIT HATH NOT FLESH AND BONES, AS YE SEE ME HAVE. And when he had thus spoken, he shewed them his hands and his feet. And while they yet believed not for joy, and wondered, he said unto them, Have ye here any meat? And they gave him a piece of a broiled fish, and of an honey-comb. And he took it and did eat it before them. (emphasis mine)

Consider the wording of the above Scripture passage as it appears in the New World Translation:

> …they were IMAGINING they beheld a spirit…Feel me and see, because a spirit does not have flesh and bones just as YOU behold that I HAVE. (first and third emphasis mine)

This passage should say much to the Witnesses. First of all we learn that the people to whom Christ appeared in this instance made the same mistake as the Watchtower by "supposing" or "imagining" that He was a spirit.

Secondly, we see that Jesus specifically declared that a spirit does NOT have flesh and bones LIKE HE DOES. Therefore, He is not a spirit.

Lastly, to further prove the fact that He was present in body, Jesus requested some food and proceeded to eat what was given Him. Needless to say, a spirit does not eat!

A very feeble attempt on the part of the Watchtower to "prove" that Jesus did not raise His body can be found in Luke 24. The disciples on the road to Emmaus were joined by another traveller. This "traveller" was none other than the risen Christ. But the Scriptures say that the disciples did not recognize Him.

"Ha! There you go!", say the Witnesses, "He obviously wasn't raised in His own body because His own disciples didn't even recognize Him while He walked with them!"

Sadly, this is yet another ploy of the Watchtower to which many good people slowly nod their heads in baffled agreement. But it shouldn't be.

As is so frequently the case, a more careful consideration of what the Scriptures have to say quickly puts the assertions of the Watchtower to rest. Verse 16 plainly explains why they were not able to recognize Him..."But their eyes were holden that they should not know him." The same verse in the NASV states, "But their eyes were prevented from recognizing Him."

So we see that it was not at all a matter of Jesus looking different and it was certainly not that He was in a different body as the Watchtower would have us believe. Rather, the two on the road didn't recognize Jesus simply because He purposely prevented them from doing so! (In v. 31, we read that they were in fact able to recognize Him later).

> The resurrection of Christ is not a spiritual resurrection, nor were His appearances to the disciples spiritual manifestations. He appeared to His disciples in a bodily form. THE BODY THAT WAS LAID IN JOSEPH'S TOMB CAME FORTH ON THAT FIRST EASTER MORN TWENTY CENTURIES AGO. [9] (emphasis mine)

> And, too, it would have been a piece of deception on Christ's part, for then He appeared to His disciples only in a spiritual vision and yet

---

9 Taken from THE GREAT DOCTRINES OF THE BIBLE by William Evans (enlarged edition). Used by permission, Moody Bible Institute of Chicago. Chicago, Ill., 1974, p. 86.

conveyed to their minds the impression that He appeared bodily. But the disciples were not impressible, but exceedingly skeptical, and hence were not in a mood to see visions and mistake them for fleshy realities. [10]

THE IMPORTANCE OF THE RESURRECTION.

Paul summed up the situation quite well when he declared,

> "And if Christ be not raised, your faith is vain; ye are yet in your sins." (1 Corinthians 15:17)

Dr. Lockyer has this to offer;

> The importance of Christ's victory over death cannot be too strongly stressed. 'Christianity is a religion of miracles,' says one theologian, 'and the miracle of Christ's Resurrection is the living center and object of Christian faith.' The doctrine of the Resurrection is of primary value for on it all the doctrines of grace depend. If Christ did not rise again then we are still in our sins. [11]

---

10 Taken from CHRISTIAN THEOLOGY, Systematic and Biblical. By Emery H. Bancroft. Grand Rapids, Michigan. Published by Zondervan Publishers, 1976, p. 135. With permission of Baptist Bible College & Seminary.

11 Taken from ALL THE DOCTRINES OF THE BIBLE by Herbert Lockyer. Copyright 1964 by the Zondervan Publishing House. Used by permission. p. 53.

Those that know and serve the Lord are fully aware that He is almighty and that nothing is too difficult for Him. Why then do the cults insist that Jesus' body was irreversibly dead?

The natural man views death as a final state which mankind can do nothing to change. However, those who are in Christ realize that their faith is in the One Who has the very power of life and death. We must not limit what He can do. For if the Giver of Life Himself is subject unto eternal and permanent death, whether in body or spirit, how then can we trust our eternity to Him?

HOW TO KNOW JESUS

If what you have read on the preceding pages has caused you to re-examine your previously-held beliefs or theories, I encourage you to consider inviting the Lord Jesus Christ into your heart and life right now.

Jesus Himself clearly said that the only way to heaven was to be born again (See John 3:3; 3:5; 3:7). Won't you accept what He has said and done for you?

HOW TO BE BORN AGAIN

To be born again simply means to accept Jesus Christ into your heart and life and make Him Lord over your life. To do this, simply pray to Him and invite Him into your life and ask Him to forgive your sins. You must be sincere when you pray, you can't fool God.

A SAMPLE PRAYER

Dear Lord,

I am a sinner (Romans 3:10; 3:23).

I recognize that Jesus died for me and that He rose from the dead on the third day. I ask that He come into my life right now and forgive me of all my sin.

Help me to know your will Lord, and to follow it.

I ask this in Jesus' name.

Amen

WHAT NOW?

Now that you're born again (John 6:37), it's imperative that you pray and read your Bible everyday. You should also find a solid, Bible-believing church to attend.

Bibliography

Bancroft, Emery H. CHRISTIAN THEOLOGY. Grand Rapids, Michigan. Zondervan Publishing House.

Bancroft, Emery H. ELEMENTAL THEOLOGY. Grand Rapids, Michigan. Zondervan Publishing House.

Bowser, Arthur M. WHAT EVERY JEHOVAH'S WITNESS SHOULD KNOW. Denver, Colorado. Accent Publications.

Evans, William. THE GREAT DOCTRINES OF THE BIBLE. Chicago, Illinois. Moody Bible Institute.

Hutson, Curtis et al. GREAT PREACHING ON THE DEITY OF JESUS CHRIST. Murfreesboro, TN., 1986, Sword of the Lord Publishers.

Lockyer, Herbert. ALL THE DOCTRINES OF THE BIBLE. Grand Rapids, Michigan. Zondervan Publishing House.

Martin, Walter R. KINGDOM OF THE CULTS. Ventura, California. Vision House Publishers.

Martin, Walter R. MARTIN SPEAKS OUT ON THE CULTS. Ventura, California. Vision House Publishers.

Martin, Walter R. THE NEW CULTS. Ventura, California. Regal Books.

McDowell, Josh, and Don Stewart. HANDBOOK OF TODAY'S RELIGIONS: UNDERSTANDING THE CULTS. San Bernadino, California. Here's Life Publishers.

Rice, John R. THE SON OF GOD, A VERSE-BY-VERSE COMMENTARY ON THE GOSPEL ACCORDING TO JOHN. Murfreesboro, TN. Sword of the Lord Publishers.

Smeaton, George. THE DOCTRINE OF THE HOLY SPIRIT. Carlisle, Pennsylvania. Banner of Truth Trust.

Thomas, F.W. MASTERS OF DECEPTION. Grand Rapids, Michigan. Baker Book House.

Van Impe, Jack. GREAT SALVATION THEMES. Royal Oak, Michigan. Jack Van Impe Ministries.

Walvoord, John F. THE HOLY SPIRIT. Grand Rapids, Michigan. Zondervan Publishing House.

Williams, J.L. VICTOR PAUL WIERWILLE AND THE WAY INTERNATIONAL. Chicago, Illinois. Moody Bible Institute of Chicago.

Suggested Reading

Ahmanson, John Secret History – An Eyewitness account of the Rise of Mormonism. Translated by Gleason L. Archer. Moody Press, Chicago, 1984.

Berry, Harold J. Examining the Cults. Back to the Bible, Nebraska, 1979.

Boa, Kenneth Cults, World Religions and You. Victor Books, Illinois, 1983.

Breese, David Know the Marks of Cults. Victor Books, Illinois, 1975.

Dencher, Ted Why I Left Jehovah's Witnesses. Christian Literature Crusade, Pennsylvania, 1966, 1980, 1985.

Duggar, Gordon E. Watch Out for the Watchtower! Baker Book House, Michigan, 1985.

Enroth, Ronald et al A Guide to Cults and New Religions. Intervarsity Press, Illinois, 1983.

Fraser, Gordon H. Is Mormonism Christian? Moody Press, Chicago, 1977.

Geer, Thelma "Granny" Mormonism, Mama and Me. Moody Press, Chicago, 1986.

Gruss, Edmond Charles Apostles of Denial. Presbyterian and Reformed Publishing Co., 1970.

Hoekema, Anthony A. The Four Major Cults. William B. Eerdmans Publishing Co., Michigan, 1963.

McElveen, Floyd C. The Mormon Illusion. Regal Books, California, 1977, 1979.

McManus, Una, and John Cooper Dealing with Destructive Cults. Zondervan Publications, Michigan, 1984.

Martin, Walter, and Norman Klann Jehovah of the Watchtower. Bethany House Publishers, Minnesota, 1974.

Martin, Walter R. Essential Christianity. Regal Books, California, 1962, 1975, 1980.

Robertson, Irvine What the Cults Believe. Moody Press, Chicago, 1983.

Schnell, William J. Thirty Years a Watchtower Slave. Baker Book House, Michigan, 1971.

Tanner, Jerald and Sandra The Changing World of Mormonism. Moody Press, Chicago, 1980, 1981.

Trombley, Charles Bible Answers for Jehovah's Witnesses. Expositor Publications, Oklahoma, 1975.

Tucker, Bruce Twisting the Truth. Bethany House Publishers, Minnesota, 1987.

Van Baalen, J.K. The Chaos of Cults. William B. Eerdmans Publishing Co., Michigan, 1962.

Lightning Source UK Ltd.
Milton Keynes UK
UKHW022255220221
379203UK00011B/2534

9 781432 762902